T0360630

Fostering Wisdom at Work

Most people can name dozens of knowledgeable people in their private and business lives, but highly value the very limited number deemed as wise. The fields of gerontology, psychology, and social science have attempted to study the phenomena of wisdom with little significant clarity or understanding of the construct within the expansive workforce development field. Wisdom, as an important aspect of a growing global knowledge economy, lacks the frameworks and theories needed for fostering workplace wisdom.

This book brings a scholarly scrutiny to the study of wisdom, propelling the attribute to prominence within the broad field of workforce development and particularly within the growing context of a global knowledge economy. It investigates the characteristics of wisdom and offers theories, frameworks, and techniques to foster wisdom in the workplace, recognizing it as a vital key to success for individuals and society.

The ideal audience of this book includes senior learning specialists, organization development managers, HRD directors, knowledge managers, and workforce scholar-practitioners. These key individuals in organizations understand talent management and have a vested interest in the career construction of individuals in their organizations.

Jeff M. Allen is an internationally recognized scholar in the area of workforce innovation for the knowledge economy. Together with his colleagues, he prepares students for jobs that are not yet created. He serves as a Regents Professor of Information Science at the University of North Texas.

Routledge Focus on Business and Management

The fields of business and management have grown exponentially as areas of research and education. This growth presents challenges for readers trying to keep up with the latest important insights. *Routledge Focus on Business and Management* presents small books on big topics and how they intersect with the world of business.

Individually, each title in the series provides coverage of a key academic topic, whilst collectively, the series forms a comprehensive collection across the business disciplines.

Pop-Up Retail
The Evolution, Application and Future of Ephemeral Stores
Ghalia Boustani

Building Virtual Teams
Trust, Culture, and Remote Work
Catalina Dumitru

Fostering Wisdom at Work
Jeff M. Allen

Artificial Intelligence, Business and Civilization
Our Fate Made in Machines
Andreas Kaplan

For more information about this series, please visit: www.routledge.com/Routledge-Focus-on-Business-and-Management/book-series/FBM

Fostering Wisdom at Work

Jeff M. Allen

Routledge
Taylor & Francis Group

LONDON AND NEW YORK

First published 2022
by Routledge
4 Park Square, Milton Park, Abingdon, Oxon OX14 4RN

and by Routledge
605 Third Avenue, New York, NY 10158

Routledge is an imprint of the Taylor & Francis Group, an informa business

© 2022 Jeff M. Allen

British Library Cataloguing-in-Publication Data
A catalogue record for this book is available from the British Library

Library of Congress Cataloging-in-Publication Data
A catalog record has been requested for this book

ISBN: 978-0-367-89356-9 (hbk)
ISBN: 978-1-032-23213-3 (pbk)
ISBN: 978-1-003-01875-9 (ebk)

DOI: 10.4324/9781003018759

Typeset in Times New Roman
by codeMantra

To my family, friends, colleagues, students, and community that supports my efforts and fosters my wisdom.

Contents

Figures

Preface

Wisdom is a personal journey. My first memory of the word "wisdom" was spoken by Mrs. Hatton in fourth grade. It was within the phrase "Golden Pearls of Wisdom." It immediately seemed important to me. A golden pearl? Wisdom? In Ms. Hatton's world, "golden pearls of wisdom" meant "it's going to be on the test." I was an inquisitive kid – so, after school I went to investigate the Encyclopedia Britannica. The be-all and end-all of what was real and what wasn't real, to my boy mind, was covered in the Encyclopedia Britannica. It was the reference for all the facts. But, alas, Ms. Hatton's intriguing phrase wasn't found in those magnificent pages of knowledge. I was left to wonder and interpret.

Here's what I came up with. A golden pearl of wisdom. *Gold*: a standard of value that holds up over time regardless of borders, time, or economic circumstances. It's recession-proof. Gold has always been an accepted form of currency. There is a limited supply and limitless demand. *Pearl*: It begins as an irritant (usually a parasite) that is formed as a protection mechanism in an oyster, mussel, or clam. A pearl's value is created from a less than favorable start. A pearl takes time to create. They are hard to secure and again valued across cultures and time. Finally, *wisdom* is sought by many and secured by few. Highly valued and yet rarely found. We knowingly seek wisdom, but don't quite know what it will be when we seek and secure it. We find hints and attributes in those around us, and if we are lucky, we know of a wise person in our lives. We have been richly rewarded if we can find several wise people in our lifetime.

Can we find it in our own lives? The phrase a golden pearl of wisdom remained in my vernacular throughout my education and career – and that seed of wisdom was planted in the fourth grade.

Our innate desire to seek knowledge and understanding of the world around us is distinctive from human infancy. Data and information form rich soil capable of yielding knowledge while our intellect extends capability to gather, interpret, and integrate that knowledge. We have an intuitive desire to understand more about ourselves and the world that we inhabit. We crave to both find our space in a world that surrounds us and interact with people that come in and out of our daily lives. The quest for knowing is an ever-changing challenge for humans and a true puzzle for organizations and systems. This chase to know more, be more, and do more provides a catalyst for change and is the intrinsic motivation that drives human growth. Our seeking nature grows our resilience, personal belief structures, inspiration, courage, flexibility, self-awareness, and relationships.

Our personal growth throughout life is so different from any other person that we each have tremendous difficulty comprehending the uniqueness of other's life paths. However, this understanding of other trials, tribulations, challenges, and successes are critical to our own success as we leverage and rely on partnerships and relationships. We infer a tremendous amount of information from their stories and interactions with them during our personal journey. These interactions help us develop our personal traits such as patience, compassion, empathy, ethical behavior, and understanding of others.

These interactions with others in our lives and our innate desire to seek knowledge begin to weave and build our understanding of larger social structures and systems. These social, cultural, economic, and communication systems form a large environment that helps develop

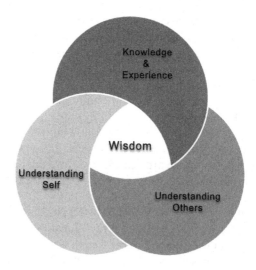

Figure 0.1 Wisdom constructs

the ability to see complex patterns, develop abstract thinking, expand insight, and work on multilevel problem-solving. We build upon wise decisions throughout our life to build our competence, confidence, and purpose and leverage our knowledge and experiences to become wiser individuals.

We *are each uniquely the same.* The purpose of Part One is to provide some insight on how to grow personal wisdom with the hope to assist others in their personal journey toward wisdom and to highlight the guiding virtues of the wise.

The purpose of Part Two is to bring better understanding of how we can mentor and build mentoring relationships to intentionally foster growth and wisdom in ourselves and others. Further, the chapters explore the importance of fostering collective wisdom within our organizations to build the knowledge, skills, and attitudes required to enhance competency and increase productivity. Wisdom is uniquely human. The path toward wisdom is challenging and worthy of our time. From birth to death, we grow our personal and collective wisdom.

Why wisdom? It's a portion of our life's journey and the best part!

Acknowledgments

The acknowledgment for any authored work can be inexhaustible. Family, friends, colleagues, students, teammates, audiences, and the random interested stranger contributed insights, posed questions, argued skepticisms, or clarified suppositions as the book developed from concept to finished manuscript.

There was a small group of sages that played key roles in moving this wisdom expedition forward to successful completion:

Denise Allen

Jared Allen

Tristan Allen

Dr. Linda Allen

Dr. Mike Allen

Max Atkinson

Mary Chandler

Ben Drezek

Hock Hockheim

Dr. Kristine Farmer

Dr. Mariya Gavrilova-Aguilar

Dr. Suliman Hawamdeh

Dr. Amanda Leibovitz

Dr. Mandolin Mull

Dr. Brian O'Connor

William Radcliffe

Dr. Pamela Scott-Bracey

Dr. Brad Shuck

Sage Research Tribe

Part One
Personal Wisdom

1 Our Personal Journey

Life Is Not Fair

All is not fair. This simple statement makes a lot of difference at how we look at ourselves and others. There is no magic wand to make everything fair. From birth to death, we encounter unfairness in our lives that impacts our ability to gain all of the success we might have otherwise realized if life had just been a bit fairer. Fairness cannot be counted upon, even in the best of circumstances.

There are many factors that have an impact on our ability to achieve at the highest levels, such as socioeconomic status, gender, culture, place of birth, ethnicity, nutrition, educational background, family structure, violence, isolation, and neglect. These factors can have a positive or negative affect on our confidence, competence, and purpose and can help or hinder our ability to succeed.

These disparities in life certainly should be addressed at the local, regional, and international levels to provide every individual a fair and equitable start in life, but addressing these disparities is well beyond what we can impact in our personal journey. So, for the moment, let's simply address that there are disparities that impact our beginning, middle, and end.

We share our life journey with many people along the way, each with shared experiences and different perspectives on how to navigate the next stages of life. However, our pathway, past, present, and future belong to us as individuals. We strive for knowledge, enhance our skills, adapt our attitudes, and build our abilities based on our individuality.

A neglectful childhood, maltreatment, malnutrition, and a low socioeconomic status can dramatically impact a person's ability to become educated and financially successful. Family structures, social environment, and education can significantly change the direction of a teenager's life and future career. Calamities, strife, war, and other

DOI: 10.4324/9781003018759-2

"acts of God" can drastically alter our access to common markers of economic and social success. Our unique journey creates a differentiation between us and every other person that ever lived – or will live. This is a scary proposition, unless we also accept that hundreds of millions of people have some of our shared life experiences. Simply put, we don't all have the same starting point, and for many, we will be redirected on our path, but it remains our path to manage.

Adversity and setbacks are unique opportunities for growth that are part of our personal life experience and journey toward wisdom. Bad circumstances (e.g., early abuses, addiction, and overcoming challenging situations) can be leveraged to help foster personal wisdom. A keystone of becoming wise is overcoming adversity, which provides another avenue to build a capacity for compassion and understanding of other's unique challenges to help them chart a course of action to overcome their own adversities. Wisdom, uniquely, is enhanced by life experiences and adversities. Wisdom is built by harnessing personal adversity and using the experience to better survive and thrive in a chaos that might overcome less prepared individuals.

This book initiates a discussion of fostering wisdom at work. The depth and breadth of this subject is too vast and academic studies are too young to comprehensively understand the subject in one book or, as has been found, even in one field of study. The study of wisdom is multidisciplinary. Since the 1990s, organizations have struggled to understand the concept of learning organizations. At the heart of wisdom is learning and unlearning. Wisdom cannot exist without learning. While great intellect is not a requirement of wisdom, it is often closely associated with wisdom in the same way that we associate age with wisdom.

This book is intended to orient individual and organizational thinking toward wisdom rather than greater learning and knowledge. All the knowledge in the world is of little use without the wisdom to create a course of action leading to beneficial and productive decisions for individuals, communities, and society.

Before we truly begin to understand wisdom, it's easier to first lay out a few beliefs. I believe the following to be true:

- Humans are complicated beings with an innate ability and desire to seek new knowledge. There are decades of research on the differences between individuals as they grow and from many biological perspectives, the dissimilarities simply can't be ignored; however, the commonality between people is overwhelming when you look at humans as a whole and not as individuals. We are uniquely the same.

- In the very broadest sense, a person's age, gender, socioeconomic background, race, cultural background, religion, weight, height, disability, or abilities do not matter. These factors certainly provide obstacles, a shortcut, a head start, or barriers in educational, social, and the workplace. But, in the area of wisdom, they provide moments of adversity, challenge, learning, compassion, deep understanding, and insight for each individual because of their uniquely diverse story. This unique diversity provides any individual with the basic ingredients needed to seek wisdom.
- Wisdom is openly accessible to all humans. Wisdom is not relegated to the young, old, rich, poor, wise, religious, well travelled, a gender, or to a culture. How long will it take to become wise? This depends on the individual. So, let's talk about humans in general rather than individuals specifically. Humans want to learn, grow, and thrive. We take this approach in our discussion to help foster wisdom.

Who Is Wise?

The difficulty in understanding wisdom is getting a good "feel" for what it is and is not. To begin our discussion of wisdom, it's important to have a vision in your mind of the word "wise." The ability to make wise decisions is unquestionably a signal that a person has attributes of a wise person, but wise decisions don't necessarily create a wise person. We are not talking about wise decisions that are made in our daily lives but the idea of becoming a wise person – a person that others would seek because of their wisdom.

A knowledgeable person may also be wise but not necessarily. Who might knowledgeable people be in our lives? Parents, family, colleagues, instructors, mentors may each be included in a list of knowledgeable people. The number and type of knowledgeable people that we know will vary widely from individual to individual.

Use your own definition of knowledge to complete the following exercise:

Consider for a few minutes the people that you personally (within the context of your personal and professional engagements) that you consider "knowleddgable". Make a list of these people for your own reference.

After completing this exercise, you may now have a list of a dozen (or more) knowledgeable individuals. Each of us likely knows many knowledgeable people. This number varies from person to person and from time to time, but, for most, the number of knowledgeable people that we know has simply become too high to count. This isn't a surprise. We interact with knowledgeable people on a regular basis in our lives whether their knowledge is wide-ranging and global, or local and subject-matter specific.

To be knowledgeable is not unique. It's common to accept that someone is knowledgeable within the context of their personal or professional lives. These knowledgeable or intelligent individuals may include our family, friends, coworkers, associates, well-known personalities, mentors, and teachers.

To be knowledgeable shouldn't be a surprise. Our formal and informal educational systems (elementary, secondary, postsecondary, and career) are very good at creating intelligent/knowledgeable people. As a society, we understand how to create and transfer knowledge. We understand the theories and models of how to transfer knowledge to both learners and our peers.

In general, knowledge can be demonstrated in two major forms:

Explicit knowledge is knowledge that others know. This is often referred to as book knowledge. It is knowledge that can be articulated, documented, and shared efficiently.

Implicit/Tacit knowledge is knowledge of things without knowing how you know them. This is often referred to as intuitive knowledge or know-how. This is knowledge that is largely based on experience, intuition, and insight.

Use your own definition of wisdom to complete the following:

Consider for a few minutes the people that you know personally (within the context of your personal and professional engagements) that you consider "wise".

Make a list of these people for your own reference.

This second exercise is much harder and delivers fewer results. When left to our own devices to identify individuals that match the picture of wise, we become very discerning. We distinctly discriminate between wise people and knowledgeable people. Our discrimination between knowledgeable and wise considers many traits outside of simply knowledge and experience.

Typically, we begin narrowing our list of knowledgeable people down to a select few that are both knowledgeable and wise. However, often we include other people on the list that don't necessarily meet our definition of intelligent but have a wisdom that can't be denied.

Wise is more than "to know a lot." Individuals normally start with the first list of knowledgeable people and start whittling the list down to a few very special people. But, why?

Wisdom includes perspective and the ability to make sound judgments, while knowledge is simply knowing. Wisdom is a cherished trait given/bestowed on people, rather than an implicit status or stage reached. Even amongst those who are close to us as family, friends, and colleagues, we may not be able to name one person that we consider wise, much less more than a handful. The one(s) that we do consider wise are almost always spoken of with cherished prose that go far beyond their knowing.

There are considerations as to who we, as a collective, consider wise. From this standpoint, let's point out a few exemplar individuals that have been widely recognized for their remarkable wisdom.

Maya Angelou	Winston Churchill
Marie Curie	Daryl Davis
Ann Frank	Mahatma Gandhi
Martin Luther King, Jr.	Abraham Lincoln
Nelson Mandela	Theodore Roosevelt
Mother Teresa	Wangarī Maathai
Malala Yousafzai	

These names may be surprising. This is not a list of perfect people, nor is it a comprehensive list of the remarkably wise. Your list of remarkably wise people might look different. Visualizing the attributes of a wise person is often the first step in understanding why we consider them wise. This sample provides help in developing a picture of what wise means to you. Wise does not mean perfect. Each of the individuals on the list will have their own list of critics. As a collective, however, this list helps us understand the concept of globally/remarkably wise.

Wise is subjectively defined and based on local engagement with individuals (locally wise). There's nothing wrong with this subjectiveness; the title of wise is freely given by those who interact with an individual. In addition to individual determination of wise, there is a community or societal recognition of wise individuals. These same individuals might be remarkably or globally wise and receive widespread recognition of their wisdom. It only depends on the shared values that we have with those considered wise. Without shared, and sometimes universal, values it would be hard for a person to reach that state of influence.

Your personal list and the sample list of the famously wise provide a foundation to begin structuring your own personal profile of the wise. In addition, consider this list of behavioral characteristics and traits that are woven in virtually every discussion on the topic of identifying the wise:

Understanding Self	*Knowledge and Experience*	*Understanding Others*
Agency	Abstract reasoning	Accountable
Belief system	Competent	Benevolent
Courageous	Explicit knowledge	Compassionate
Driven	Implicit knowledge	Empathetic
Flexible	Insightful	Ethical
Mindful	Intuitive	Generous
Optimistic	Learner	Influential
Patient	Objective	Inspiring
Perseverant	Perceptive	Listener
Self-directed	Sound judgment	Responsible
Self-growth	Systematic thinking	Sacrificing
Self-reliant	Unlearning	Sharing

While not every wise person has all these characteristics, they are often used to describe both the locally and globally wise. We will discuss many of these characteristics as we discuss wisdom.

> *The list above provides a starting point for characteristics of the wise.*
> *Who are the wise people in your world?*
> *Why do you personally consider them wise?*
> *What traits are shared between the individuals?*
> *What traits are unique among the individuals?*
> *Use the above profile to help you better understand your personal list of wise people.*

The wise people in our lives serve to influence continued growth and path toward wisdom. They are our wise mentors – due not only to their knowledge but also from a mix of personal characteristics that influence others.

Our personal lists of wise individuals are valued for their sound judgment, ethics, and influence in our personal lives. Your personal list of knowledgeable people may number in the hundreds. Knowledge is not unique – our societies are very well versed in producing knowledgeable people. On the other hand, each of our lists of wise people is most likely less than a half-dozen people – they are our golden pearls.

We Are Each Uniquely the Same

There are many different theories, models, frameworks, and processes in the relatively young field of wisdom science, yet there are few solid and undisputed answers. What else can we expect from a term that is so hard to simply define? It's easier to begin the discussion with an analogy:

The building of personal wisdom could be described as a puzzle:

A unique **puzzle** that each of us constructs piece-by-piece to slowly be completed with each year's experiences, each hour of living, each minute of our senses, moments of insight, and instances of influence that touch our lives. The construction of our personal puzzle begins far sooner than our own self-awareness, and, if we are lucky, to the last moments of our story's end.

Pieces of the puzzle we collect vary individually and with some pieces dark and ugly, deep and meaningful, clear and crisp, brief, simple, uplifting, or inconsequential. However, any one of these pieces can be life-altering. Each experience brings a different texture to our story and provides composition and foundation that we will later build on. We certainly have keystone pieces that direct our life path (for better or worse). There is no picture to follow, no special shape or size. It's creation and the resulting form of our puzzle will change over time.

These pieces vary in importance, in placement, and value. Some puzzle pieces are simply missing and need to be self-created. Sadly, or happily, some of the values and placements are often not our choice but chosen for us. Circumstances of our childhood home are most often out of our individual control. We can't control our family's socio-economic status, location, mental health, structure, and a multitude of other impacts on our formative years. In our adult lives, traumas happen that we must overcome, or boons are found that can be leveraged. We certainly struggle to find the meaning of events and struggle to find how they help us. The interesting and unusual part of completing this puzzle is that each of us gets to create and place many of the puzzle pieces that create our story.

Think about this puzzle differently, not as a static form out of the box but as a living entity that we manipulate throughout our lifetime. We have the ability to adapt puzzle pieces that create the final picture of our life. As children and as adults, we have barriers intentionally or unintentionally placed in front of us and circumstances that hold us from the best of our dreams and goals, yet, as individuals, we choose our responses and change the fit of our puzzles. Our childhood circumstances, adversities, barriers, triumphs, and tragedies can help to form us as different, and better, individuals.

To foster wisdom, we have to learn from adversity and challenge, previous experience, and the knowledge and experiences of others. Think of yourself as having wizard powers to transform and manipulate pieces, a puzzle piece creator, we are the masters with a strong hand in manipulating our final picture. We can experience, learn, unlearn, adapt, change, and create.

We each have the choice of intentionally seeking wisdom, but it is not often sought intentionally. We are only seldom taught by our mentors that wisdom is a worthy goal for each of us. It's often seen as something that will be garnered with age and experience. We often consider wisdom an unreachable goal for ourselves at the time (if ever) and relegate "the path" to wisdom to people far more worthy than ourselves. If we do intentionally seek to become wise, we then accept that wisdom as a life quest that we may never reach – if we ever even had a chance.

Discrimination-Free Wisdom

"Wise" is free of discrimination or prejudice. There are no age requirements. Wisdom science has provided evidence that there is little correlation between age and wisdom. It's important to note that we can grow wisdom at a different rate than we age. Older doesn't (necessarily) mean wiser. There is no educational requirement – while some minimal level of knowledge or intelligence is a necessary base to growing wisdom, intelligent or knowledgeable does not mean wise. There are no race or cultural requirements to become wise. We have many references and examples of wisdom (or the wise) across all cultures and throughout time.

There is no religious or nonreligious requirement for developing wisdom. Religious and nonreligious texts throughout time have studied the topic of wisdom. Wisdom is contextual with a group, community, or society. There is no ownership of the subjects, only lenses that are used to explore and grow in wisdom.

There is no location/geographic requirement for wisdom. Historians of society and linguists can provide evidence of the study and examples of wisdom from very simple to very complex societal locations. We find examples of wise people in every culture throughout our human history describing individuals as diverse as our global population. The title of "wise" is not easily earned by individuals. It is bequeathed without regard to age, race, sex, orientation, culture, religious belief, disability, citizenship, political belief, societal condition, or any other classification. It is equally accessible by all.

Wisdom is mutually respected and beneficial to society. The value of wisdom is so overwhelming that individuals ignore and overlook many discriminatory prejudices to seek the wise.

A Beginning

To begin any discussion, we need to have some common understanding of words and meanings. While there are no universal truths, we need to lay a foundation of *language* before we start any in-depth conversation. This provides both the author and the reader some common understanding – *this doesn't mean agreement* but a place to start a conversation about a little-understood and often neglected subject that so many seek: Wisdom.

In the following section, we explore some terms that may be common in our lexicon. Each term has been defined in different ways based on the field of study, or local utilization. The following is simple to provide a common starting point for further exploration.

The purpose is to provide a foundational understanding of a subject that will be more deeply explored as we move forward in the discussion of wisdom.

Feelings/Thoughts and Action

Cognitive behavioral therapy provides a wealth of understanding about the relationship between thoughts, feelings, and behaviors. We know from research that we produce three things from our emotions: thoughts, feelings, and behaviors.

Emotions come from the deepest part of every individual. They are so much a part of who we are they cannot be ignored. Emotions that stem from internal and external experiences manifest as sad, happy, afraid, hurt, confident, surprised, tired, angry, self-conscious, motivated, or strong. Each of these emotions evokes a variety of thoughts that create feelings, and these feelings provide positive or negative energy. Our unconscious emotions are the base from which feelings, thoughts, and behaviors are derived.

Thoughts are a link between our emotions and feelings. They are our ideas, perceptions, beliefs, attitudes, and opinions about ourselves, others, our communities, and societies. Our thoughts provide the ability to make sense of the world around us. These thoughts account for our needs and desires, and provide us an ability to plan. What we think affects our feelings and behaviors. They allow us to manipulate data and information and conceptualize creative solutions to problems that impact our emotions, feelings, and thoughts through a set of actions or behaviors (Figure 1.1).

Feelings are a conscious product of our emotions based on our personal experience. How we feel affects what we think and what we do. Afraid is a feeling that is based on a fearful emotion then regulated through our thoughts into a conscious experience.

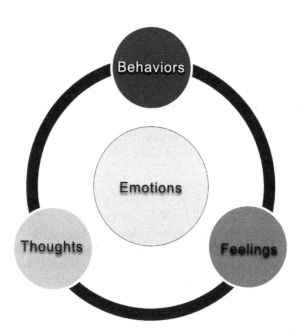

Figure 1.1 Emotion cycle.

Behavior is an observable action. We may act directly from an emotional level with no thought of consequences or thoughtfully through creative solutions. Our behaviors affect the way that we feel and think.

It's difficult for us to make great strides when we are pulled in a positive or negative direction by the feeling of anger, contentment, fear, or sadness. Feelings, thoughts, and behaviors can pull us in different directions or enable us to be guided, in concert, toward a goal.

Learning

Education encompasses creative, replicable, and effective strategies, techniques, tools, and systems used to efficiently enhance the knowledge acquisition process for learners. There is a tremendous amount of room to argue the theories and techniques of teaching, learning, and knowledge acquisition. As learners, we seek context – the comfort of fitting new knowledge into the neat cupboards, drawers, and cabinets of our minds. Of course, some use stack and piles, rather than file cabinets and folders. Our context of the world changes during the minutes, seconds, years, and decades of our learning and experiences.

Formal learning is typically viewed as structured as classroom learning with a "sage of the stage" and learners in the seats. This ideal view of learning structure extended from our early childhood classrooms to graduate seminars. Even as employees transitioned to work, our learning model continued for the most part in the way of training classrooms where a familiar style and structure is presented to meet our expectation of education.

Learning is a natural intellectual process of acquiring and enhancing knowledge, skills, attitudes, and ability through education, observation, self-study, experience, and experimentation. Too often overlooked is our self-learning outside of the classroom. Undocumented on any learning transcripts is the education that we received from individuals in our lives from family, friends, and community (e.g., cleaning, cooking, chores, schedules) to social interactions with others (e.g., sports, religious services, visits to extended family, vacations, and overnighters at friends' houses). This is a substantial education and is often more impactful to structuring our lifetime behavioral characteristics, traits, and emotional intelligence (e.g., compassion, communication, belief structures, respect, morals, trust).

In the 21st century, learning structures have dramatically changed, especially in higher education and work. Secondary and postsecondary education has moved from a "sage on the stage" toward encouraging self-learning and discovery. No longer is education relegated to the classroom on the singular knowledge of a teacher. As E.O. Wilson states in his 1998 book *Consilience: The Unity of Knowledge*, "The world henceforth will be run by synthesizers, people able to put together the right information at the right time, think critically about it, and make important choices wisely." Synthesis and self-learning, in the 21st century, is a modality of learning rarely imagined in the mid-20th-century school.

Models of learning are vast. The key to learning in the 21st century continues toward "self": self-direction, self-regulation, self-planning, self-teaching, self-education, self-management, self-guiding, self-instruction, self-reflection, and self-evaluation. This does not mean that there is a decline in the art and science of education. It simply means that self-learning behavior is inherent when there is expanding information that is accessible to learners.

While there is a significant difference in structured vs. unstructured learning, it is something that must be addressed in the learning environment as we move through the next few decades. Our learning and training models of the last century have become antiquated with the information age. The teacher and trainer will be *replaced* as we move through the next three decades. Ok, not replaced. They will be repositioned to a role of facilitator in the learning and training processes.

Progress and Growth

Performance is an often measured and poorly designed aspect of our daily and work lives. Performance encompasses creative, replicable, and effective strategies geared toward reaching desired goals through human behavioral change and measurement of this change. The measurement of this performance is conducted in two major ways: formative and summative evaluations. For this discussion, let's look at formative evaluation rather than summative.

Formative evaluation is conducted with the main intent to measure how performance has increased or declined from one point to another. This type of evaluation is ongoing and often overlooked as we live our daily lives. This evaluation may be as simple as our morning stretch as we get out of bed (indicating if it's going to be a good day, or not), glance at the gas gauge, speedometer, daily planner, or a to-do list. In a classroom or training room, this could be questions from an instructor to assess understanding, daily worksheets, or homework. Human performance is seldom steady or consistent. Our performance ebbs and flows from day-to-day performance. Even at the highest levels, a world-class athlete can never stay on a "cutting edge" of performance.

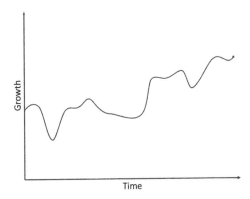

Figure 1.2 Learning and growth.

While they train for a particular day, event, or even season, it's quickly observed that there is an offseason for introspection, evaluation, modifications, remolding, and retraining to get ready for the next season (Figure 1.2).

Within the workplace we often ignore human growth, and, therefore, higher levels of performance are likely to be obtained by performance intervention and innovations leading to performance improvement. Human performance potential is limitless but must be self-designed, self-planned, self-implemented, self-evaluated, and self-evolved in a cyclical process with a plan toward growth.

Formative evaluation is key to assessing our intermittent stages of progress whether the progress is positive or negative. Negative does not necessarily mean bad progress. In a learning environment, it is often moments that we are integrating new knowledge and understanding into our existing backpack of ideas, theories, and models. While these "snapshots" of knowledge may demonstrate a retreat in understanding, we often need our current ideas questioned, examined, and revised so that we can progress at an accelerated rate. Formative evaluations are simply a progress indicator and of little value until they are examined over time.

Progress is a worthy goal. There is an inherent desire for us to compare ourselves to others, however, we each progress at a different pace. We must recognize that all progress is not straightforward, and we are not always necessarily progressive in our planned steps. Progress is to move forward toward a destination over time or distance.

The Lens

The expansive subject of wisdom has been discussed throughout history by scholars in every different field. Without exception, there has been the same conclusion: We know what wisdom is, but we don't know the formula to achieve it, and it is very difficult to measure. Have there been people that have become wise? Certainly. There are remarkably wise people that live on our planet that, as a collective, we point to them as being "wise." Philosophers have struggles to understand what exactly wisdom means and to some extent to how it can be obtained. Religious scholars have endeavored to find enlightenment. Maslow's hierarchy of needs even touches the subject of religion, stating that, after other needs are fulfilled, humans have the *need* for self-actualization.

As you investigate the study of wisdom you will find an endless collection of definitions, an endless collection of experiences, and an endless set of prose describing "what is wise." At another part of this collection of literature, academic and nonacademic, you will find a vast amount of subject matter on "how to make wise choices." The subject of how to make wise choices is much more common and provides us with a much closer understanding of everyday behaviors that lead to wisdom.

The subject of this book is fostering wisdom. The choice of title is important but even more so with when the subject is wisdom. This book is written through the lens of social science rather than psychology or philosophy. The lens of different disciplines clash. This clash does not mean that one is right, and another is wrong. Each discipline is approaching the problem in a different way. This is analogous to a climber looking at El Capitan. There are many ways to summit the mountain. Each must be evaluated within the context of the climber and their abilities.

Early in the training of educators and trainers like me, we were taught to teach so that others can learn. This approach works for 98% of our subjects. Wisdom is one of the subjects in 2%. Wisdom is a journey of self-awareness, self-control, self-learning, and self-reflection. We can teach individuals where to find data (fact, figures, measurements, and signals). We can teach individuals to provide context to that data to create information (understanding relationships, organization, structured, and usefulness of data). We can teach knowledge (understanding patterns and meaning from information, ideas, synthesization, and conceptualization with an outcome of learning).

Suddenly we come to a barrier as educators and trainers. We can no longer teach beyond the level of knowledge. Wisdom cannot be given or taught from one person to the next. It's earned via a journey of self-awareness, self-control, self-learning, and self-reflection. We cannot teach insight, understanding of principles, belief structure, courage, discernment, drive, empathy, insight, inspiration, integrity, morals, perseverance, respect, responsibility, sacrifice, systematic understanding, trust, understanding of others, or understanding of self.

I argue that we must move ourselves from a teacher-oriented approach toward a learner-oriented approach of investigation and discovery. A teacher moves from an authoritarian role of "sage on the stage" to a role of coach, mentor, motivator, or witness with the goal of encouraging, providing, or remediating to create a course of action that will lead the learner to make the self-discovery of beneficial and productive decisions for individuals, communities, and society.

As a 30-year+ scholar, educator, trainer, and coach I will readily admit that there is no clear avenue to teach someone wisdom in the same way that we convey the spectrum of data, information, and knowledge. Wisdom is a subject that can only be fostered, and wisdom is very different in every individual. Wisdom is fostered within a person and is supplemented and enhanced through formal and informal mentoring experiences.

We value wisdom. We interact with many knowledgeable yet too few wise people who influence our lives. We know what wisdom is when we see it, but the path to achieve that same level of wisdom is shrouded in questions. It's an area that must be explored as a unique human trait that is too seldom achieved in our communities, societies, and workplaces.

Defining Wisdom

There are too many definitions provided by history to prescribe a singular correct definition that is accepted by any field or individual. The title of "wise" is gifted with context and observation of a person's characteristics, actions, and behavior as through the eyes of people around them. Wisdom has characteristics, traits, and behavioral profiles that can be observed and measured within the growing field of wisdom science. Wisdom is a pinnacle state of human development and a uniquely human quality.

Personification assigns human characteristics to nonhumans that mimic human traits and behaviors. The wise wolf (counsel, trust, intuition), wise owl (education, intellect), or wise raven (discerning intelligence) are examples of our personification of animals. It's easy to transfer wise characteristics to animals. Wisdom has yet to be duplicated in other creatures or in artificial intelligence (AI).

Consider, again, your personal list of wise people (our unique golden pearls). Consider their compassion, influence, abstract thinking, belief structure, intuition, explicit knowledge, personal agency, and insight. In all cases, our personification of a wise wolf or AI pales in comparison to traits and characteristics of the valuable people on our personal list of wise people.

In the realm of artificial intelligence, it is improbable that wisdom can be replicated. Personification might be possible, but it will again pale in comparison to human wisdom. Insight provides us the ability to reflect, assess, and overcome barriers to understanding, learning, and communicating. Our personal self-assessment and self-awareness are critical components to developing characteristics such as systematic understanding, self-control, belief structures, and ethical behavior. Sound judgment is harvested from life experience, learning, observation, failure, and overcoming adversity. Sound judgment is based on available data, information, and knowledge that are sourced at the time of decisions. A unique aspect of the wise that is often mentioned is that there is not always a provided answer when asked but rather a course of action. This course of action must be made with multiple layers of individuals, communities, and systems addressed to determine impact beyond the individual, beyond intelligence and knowledge.

Together, we'll proceed with the following definition of wisdom:

> Wisdom is a uniquely human virtue combining compassion, intuition, knowledge, experience, and sound judgment to create a beneficial course of action for individuals, communities, and society.

2 Knowledge, Experience, and Age

Age and Wisdom

Wisdom is a uniquely human accomplishment and process that is overwhelmingly misunderstood as an outcome of aging. There is often an assumption that with age comes wisdom. In other words, as we grow older, we will also become wiser. This would mean that the inherent experience that individuals collect during their lifetime of experience would create a finality of wisdom. If this were the case, everyone that we can name that is a certain age would be wise. It's not incorrect to say that we grow wiser with age, but it can't be assumed that with age we will all become wise.

We will gain knowledge, understanding, and experience as a natural activity during our childhood, careers, family activities, trials, and tribulations, but does this necessarily lead us, as individuals, to wisdom? Research would argue that there is little to no correlation between age and wisdom. If there was a strong connection between wisdom and age, we would have a plethora of older wise people in our lives. To investigate this idea, we need to start with a better understanding of age since it's most often associated with our birthdays – our chronological age.

Growing Up

In our childhood, we have very little control of what impacts our day-to-day life. Research shows that many lifetime traits are formed in late adolescents and early adulthood. Personality traits may be constrained or revealed based on family, social environments, and levels of personal maturity. Personality traits are persistent patterns of feeling, thinking, and behaving across time (e.g., adventurousness, compassion, flexibility, drive, impatience, self-awareness, narcissism).

DOI: 10.4324/9781003018759-3

This does not mean that traits and behavior characteristics cannot be changed. Personality traits can be slowly changed and adapted across a lifetime. We have many examples of humans turning their lives around and moving away from negative behaviors. These changes may come from maturity, growth and understanding or a simple desire to improve, learn, grow, and age.

As children and adolescents, we grow and learn in a wide variety of households with a never-ending possibility of family structures (e.g., intergenerational, traditional, or single-parent homes) that affect our family mentoring structures for the better or worse. In addition to these structures, we have issues of various levels of childcare, welfare services, child healthcare, and economic support that can greatly affect the mentoring structures. Socioeconomic conditions in adolescence can restrict or enhance access to helpful resources. Severe social and health problems can have a further impact ranging from homelessness, substance abuse, mental health, neglect and abuse, and many other problems that can endanger life.

The difficulty in our exploration of wisdom is not necessarily traits but influential activities in our lives that have long-term impact that may constrain our ability to express certain traits and characteristics. We can't get rid of these influences, large and small, but we do have to recognize and leverage the positive and negative impacts to our lives as we continue our journey. It would be wonderful to say we can choose every turn of our path in life. Yes, we certainly have choices, but sometimes a portion of our path is chosen for us by our early experiences, socioeconomic conditions, medical situations, and other adversities.

This highlights a variety of issues that influence our early life that are outside our ability to influence. Many of the circumstances of our youth can have a long-term positive or negative influence on how we value many of the wisdom traits. Our experiences can enhance understanding, extend compassion, raise generosity, bias morals, lower optimism, impact trust, increase personal agency, or increase aspirations.

Positive early experiences as a positive correlate to future success. Conditions such as family stability, higher socioeconomic status, educational opportunities, and excellence in support services are highly sought as conditions that provide a solid foundation to success in life, at least as measured by conventional measurements of success. These stable and positive childhood environments certainly have advantages and are preferable for most. These environments provide a "rich soil" for growing knowledge. Just like a greenhouse, a safe and contained environment allows plants to thrive in a safe environment.

On the other hand, negative early experiences shape the majority of some people's stories. We know that not everyone can or does grow up in an exemplary safe and positive environment. Unlike a greenhouse, the world has many plants that grow and thrive in a hostile environment that challenges every fiber of the plant. Wind, sun, humidity, moisture is no longer controlled. We know these wild plants thrive in both adverse and comfortable environments.

While overwhelming adversity can lead to disaster, overcoming adversity fosters our wisdom. Self-learning from our early lives, the process of adaptation, applying old lessons to new situations, reflection on our past, and our readiness to unlearn the old models to learn new models are enhanced by our ability to overcome adversity and strive for betterment. Adversity is a key to becoming wise; we don't become hardy in comfort.

Defining Age

We first divide age into two broad categories, childhood and adulthood. These are the categories that we use when we talk about people's age. Many of our developmental theories are divided and applied to these two broad categories of a person's life. After dividing people into these two categories, the next natural division is chronological *age*. Our birthdays tell us how many years we've lived on this blue marble. However, our chronological age doesn't provide much of an understanding of our individual psychological, biological, and social development. To comprehend more about aging, we need to reflect on a little about how we can measure age. This provides a better understanding of why chronological age is not a predictor of wisdom.

When we describe chronological age (number of years since birth), we have a very good comparative measurement across people. The CDC describes eight chronological age categories for children to understand developmental milestones:

> Infants (0–1 years)
> Toddlers (1–2 years)
> Toddlers (2–3years)
> Preschoolers (3–5 years)
> Middle Childhood (6–8 years)
> Middle Childhood (9–11 years)
> Young Teens (12–14 years)
> Teenagers (15–17 years)

Adults are general divided into three major chronological age categories:

> Young Adult (18–35 years)
> Middle-aged Adults (36–55 years)
> Older Adults (55+ years)

Finally, the field of gerontology further divides older adults into three chronological age categories:

> Youngest-old (65–74 years)
> Middle-old (75–84 years)
> Oldest-old (85+ years)

While these categories help us divide adults into 14 separate categories or stages of aging, it doesn't provide a comprehensive picture of humans as they age. The process of aging is complicated, and the question of "How old are you?" is much more complicated than counting the number of birthdays that you've celebrated.

"How old are you?" can be measured in four major ways: chronological, biological, psychological, and social. Most interesting, you can have a very different age on each of these four evaluative measures. Often, the question of *"How old do you feel?"* is a much better gauge than the number of birthdays you've celebrated.

> *Chronological age* is the number of years that we have lived since birth. It's the number of days, months, or years you have been alive without regard to health and other factors. Everyone chronologically ages at the same rate.

Biological age is the functional capability of your body's systems. Some of the factors that determine biological age include blood glucose levels, aerobic capacity (VO_2), blood pressure, muscle strength and immune functions. Everyone biologically ages at different rates. We've all met people who appear much younger or older than they really are. Some people age very rapidly, while others age at a much more gradual rate. How we age biologically is primarily influenced by genetics and is beyond our control, but it can be influenced by external factors (e.g., diet, exercise, stress, sleep, smoking, disease, or other disorders) (Figure 2.1)

Psychological age is the cognitive ability and capacity when compared to others of the same chronological age. A person's psychological age can exceed their chronological age. Often this is demonstrated in an ability that exceeds chronological age. Some of the factors

Your VO₂ Max is **46** which is excellent for men ages 50-59. Your fitness age is **20**. That's the **top 15%** for your age and gender.

Figure 2.1 VO$_2$ max as a biological age indicator.

that can impact psychological age include memory, cognitive ability and capacity, emotional stability, personal agency, self-esteem, self-efficacy, learning, and unlearning.

Social Age is the social life that you live compared to others of the same chronological age. This is measured by comparing your social roles and habits to other individuals in your age group. A person's social age can greatly vary from their chronological age. This might be viewed in terms of the chronological age at which you reach the socially expected stage of life for education, relationships, or points along a career path. Some of the factors that impact social age include lifestyle that are related to family, work, and society.

We can measure our age with many different combinations, the functional age of a person "How old do you feel?" can vary widely when you account for these four different measurements of age. These four different gauges of age are much more interdependent and provide a richer picture to our commonly held view of age. Do we mature with Age? Certainly. We mature and gain experience with age, but not everyone will grow at the same speed, garner the same experience, or flourish under the same conditions.

Age as an Approach

The number one held belief, via our historically collected stories, is the idea that age is the way to be wise. Research has shown there is no correlation between chronological age and wisdom. However, ignoring all other factors, we consider chronological age as a first indicator of wisdom. If someone is older, they must be wiser. Yes, the best way to describe it is that wisdom likely comes easier with age due to the indelible mark that perspective and experience leave on our personal understanding of the world.

There's no formula or of specific calculation for wisdom, it would be comforting to declare:

$$\text{Wisdom} = \text{trait}_1 + \text{trait}_2 + \text{trait}_2$$

We know from academic research that the personality traits, behavioral characteristics, and overall profile of wisdom are unique to an individual. Everyone's individual path to achieve a level of wisdom is also very different from person to person.

We are all uniquely the same. We'll look at individuals as a whole rather than with a singular behavioral profile that will achieve wisdom. This provides a richer look into the development of wisdom and the pathways individuals might travel that can foster that development.

Age is much more complicated than chronological age. Chronological, psychological, social, and biological aspects create an image of age that is much more complex than any birthday party might reflect. It's difficult to celebrate someone's 29th chronological age birthday, while also celebrating her 38th social birthday, her 45th psychological birthday, and 21st biological milestone. A birthday party celebrating four different age classifications each year sounds crazy, but it provides a better look at the complex picture of a person's actual age, and the dramatic effect different measurements of age might have on a person's ability to grow wise.

Wisdom and Old

Humans have collectively adopted archetypes of the old wise man, old wise woman in our cinema, stories, and fairy tales (e.g., Yoda, the Fairy Godmother, Gilda, and Gandalf). These stories and characters are helpful to understanding wisdom and become a mirror through which we can pattern our behaviors.

Our stories and fables tell us of wise old women or men. Their backs bent from a lifetime of hard work, kind yet clear eyes, a reflective mood, an inherent and deep understanding of our thoughts, a resolute understanding of the ways of the world, influence, mentorship, and often a mystic stoicism indicative of reflective thought. Yes, in many cases there is also self-imposed isolation for study or a description of their wide travel with different cultures. The characters of these stories are described not only by their vivid description of beauty, power, or intelligence but also by their virtues and experiences of understanding, caring, hardship, experience, and reputation for renowned wisdom. They are not self-described as wise but are seen as wise by their peers and those who they mentor, advise, and guide.

These character descriptions are wide and varied, but we can come to see very common themes that come alive in the stories of this wise and learned mentor. For many, the stories provide our first childhood vision of wisdom. These childhood descriptions provide us a feeling for the person, rather than simply a visual characterization of the heroic characters. The visions created of the wise become a written/visual picture of wisdom rather than a description of the age of a person. The age of the person just simply is.

Seldom do we find, in our stories, a wise, young man or woman that is just beginning life. Why? Experience. We need experience to become wise. Do we need age to be wise? Maybe, but not always; Experience counts.

> Malala Yousafzai was born in 1997 in Pakistan as the daughter of a schoolteacher (of an all-girl school). She had a love for schools that was taken away from her at age eleven due to the fact the fundamentalist took control of the Swat Valley where she and her family lived. The extremist beliefs included banning music, television, and the opportunity of girls to go to school. By 2012, Malala was already an outspoken advocate for girls' right to go to school and achieve an education. In 2012, gunmen boarded her bus, she was identified and shot in the side of the head. After ten days, she awoke to the world knowing her name and story. She and her family moved to the UK, and she continued to work toward her fight for every girl to go to school. In 2014, Malala received the Nobel Peace Prize and was distinguished as the youngest-ever Nobel laureate.

The story of Malala details a strong, young woman with an innate ability to discern critical issues with a courage well beyond her age. Malala has continued to demonstrate empathy for girls with little educational opportunities by seeing patterns and influencing opinion makers at a multinational level. For a minute, consider forgetting Malala's age and consider her experience. The amount of "experience" gained by a young inquisitive girl in a war-torn country in a valley controlled by religious extremists. There are many people that live a lifetime and don't see the violence, political extreme, and religious extreme that she encountered in her first 14 years of life. The wisdom of this young woman certainly grows exponentially as she broadens her views on the world. She has now completed her Philosophy, Politics, and Economics degree at Oxford.

Consider street urchins. Children of the streets that grow up without anything. Their experience living in this environment can include insecurity, lack of nutrition, belonging, moral foundations, and educational opportunities, and barriers to achieving greater self-esteem and living to a higher potential. Other children have never had to be without. They grew up in a secure home, a plethora of food choices, a solid family structure, friends, an ethical upbringing, and access to top-class public and private schools. They face very few barriers to achieving self-esteem and living to a higher potential.

If you consider both sets of children, the experiences from birth to 18 years old could not be any more different. Is their experience equally valuable? Maybe. Are their experiences the same? Absolutely not. Experiences are moments in time, snapshots of living that we use to move our lives in different directions. What if the people were switched? What if we changed the people, yet left the circumstances the same? Our individual interaction with each event of our life changes us in a manner that is uniquely our own. While there are certainly emotional commonalities that can be attached to great events in a person's life, we simply don't know how particular deviations change a singular individual when compared to another.

Experiences happen to everyone. We live in a sensory interactive world that brings us experiences or we personally seek experiences. Experiences provide each of us an opportunity to find meaning and learning. What we do with each experience matters. We apply our insight to fuse new experiences to old experiences and make sound judgments to move forward. As we foster wisdom, we must work to gain from experiences – good or bad.

While experience and knowledge are gained from age, wisdom is gained not only from this experience but also from thoughtful and planned experiences for purposeful learning, education, and growth. Wisdom is a uniquely human accomplishment and process that is overwhelmingly misunderstood as an outcome of aging. Wisdom has characteristics, traits, and behavioral profiles that can be observed and measured within the growing field of wisdom science. With this measurement, we have the opportunity to measure growth, create goals, build experiences, and develop a profile for ourselves and others that demonstrate wisdom beyond information, knowledge, and experience.

Wise and Young

Our path toward wisdom, individually, is truly a race against time. We only have so much time on this planet with our, hopefully, 100 years of life. If we accept the premise that growing wiser is a goal, we must ask a lot of questions: How can we leverage our experiences and knowledge to build our depth and breadth of wisdom? How can we build out experiences in adversity? How do we foster understanding of complex situations? How do we survive challenges and take advantage of upheavals and overwhelming setbacks to build our resolve?

This, quite possibly, is the biggest personal challenge presented. For most, growing older and wiser is an interwoven part of the human aging process and not something that we can impact individually through personal focus and mentorship. It just happens for some. It's not that we don't want to grow wiser, it simply is not an inherent goal. We aren't born with an impulse or aspiration to grow our wisdom independent of age. Wisdom is a uniquely human quality that we don't understand well enough to easily find as a meaningful and attainable goal for most people rather than for a unique and small minority.

We cannot teach or be taught to be wise. However, wisdom can be fostered. Wisdom begins with wise individual choices that are often guided by our parents and guardians. Our homes are kind environments (meaning, enclosed and known), rather than wicked environments (meaning, unknown and ever changing). The adversity of walking, running, and riding a bike are learned not only through direct training but also through a series of built experiences in pulling up, toddling in the flat and relatively kind confines of a home. Hiking, climbing, and mountaineering are built on a base of knowledge that we apply to other more wicked situations as we grow. Our wise decisions of caution on slick or uneven terrain comes from experience or the learned experience of others. To extend this idea, when we are faced with an unknown situation, without assistance, we draw upon previous data, information, and learning or experience knowledge to chart a course of action for this new experience.

Our first challenge is to separate the concepts of aging and wisdom being acquired together. Wisdom can be acquired and expanded at a different rate than "default."

A   The first of the three graphs shows age and wisdom growing and a very classical view of growing wise (as default). We grow wise as we grow older. Wisdom is directly related to what we experience as part of our life, and our inherent ability grows wiser through

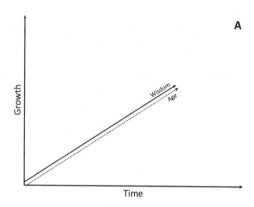

Figure 2.2 Wisdom and age in parallel.

the lessons learned during this process. In this model, experience is the driving force. As we gain more experience, we also gain wisdom. Research shows that this view of growing wise as we age is a falsehood. But it remains our default view of growing old and wise (Figure 2.2).

B This may be the most accurate view of what happens without attention (withering). Aging happens, that's a fact of life. Without attention to our depth and breadth of experience, we have a lack of events that foster the growth of wisdom, increased complacency in learning, and a muted understanding of self and others. Complacency of experience causes us to become comfortable with the same experiences time after time without personal growth. This replication, while growing the number of times we have experiences, does little to grow our wisdom.

As Oscar Wilde famously stated, "With age comes wisdom, but sometimes age comes alone."

C In a wisdom growth model, we are striving to create a wide and deep diversity of experiences and lessons learned that foster an exponential growth in personal wisdom that outruns the natural process of growing older (Figure 2.3). This requires an understanding of the behavior characteristics and traits of the wise and a systematic focus on growing in our areas of weakness. Each wise person has a mixture of unique characteristics and has a different ability to leverage each. To grow, we must keep a humble understanding of what we know and more importantly what we

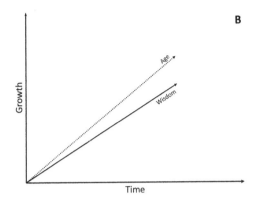

Figure 2.3 Wisdom and age-negative divergence.

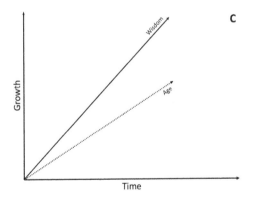

Figure 2.4 Wisdom and age-positive divergence.

do not know as we become exponentially better at self-reflection and grow in personal agency (Figure 2.4).

While these three graphs can't fully demonstrate the intricacies of aging to best reflect growth of personal wisdom, they demonstrate that age and wisdom are independent. They are not tied together. Just because a person grows older does not mean that they grow wiser.

Consider, again, this list of traits and characteristics that are inseparable from any discussion of the topic of wisdom:

Understanding Self	Knowledge and Experience	Understanding Others
Agency	Abstract reasoning	Accountable
Belief system	Competent	Benevolent
Courageous	Explicit knowledge	Compassionate
Driven	Implicit knowledge	Empathetic
Flexible	Insightful	Ethical
Mindful	Intuitive	Generous
Optimistic	Learner	Influential
Patient	Objective	Inspiring
Perseverant	Perceptive	Listener
Self-directed	Sound judgment	Responsible
Self-growth	Systematic thinking	Sacrificing
Self-reliant	Unlearning	Sharing

These traits can be observed at almost any age and have nothing to do with gender, race, culture, or socioeconomic status. These are not traits of leaders, teachers, or mentors, and they are not traits of the old. Any discussion of wisdom will find these characteristics tied inexorably to wise people in our lives.

Experience, Knowledge, Adversity, and Growth

The roles of knowledge, experience, adversity, and growth are interconnected to an extent that it's very hard to discuss one of these terms without referring to the other. Yes, each is an independent construct and it's important to understand their role in fostering wisdom. In the next sections, we'll investigate each of these terms.

Experience

Experience is the practice or the application of knowledge over a period of time. We make forward progress in our knowledge or regress in our knowledge. Experience in and of itself is neither good nor bad, it's simply a set of data/information/knowledge/evidence. We do know that life experience, especially early, can have a complicated and long-lasting effect on our behavior. Through the act of living, we collect experience. We cannot live life without experiencing it.

Each of our experiences build a tiny bit of evidence that shapes our world. As children, these experiences are very different from those collected in later life. However, if we have the same experience over and over, it is little more than looking at the same evidence again and again. Repetitive experience can garner additional insight, but, in a matter of time, you must move on to additional experiences if you wish to learn and grow.

Humans have experience throughout their life that shapes their next steps and outcome in life. Experience is gained by interaction, participation, and observation. Our experiences might be described by continuum ranging from very bad experience to very good experience and nonimpactful to life changing. Our depth and breadth of experiences both large and small can change us in very meaningful ways. Very impactful experiences may elicit strong impacts on our life decisions, yet many remain an observation or simple participation in an event. How many experiences might have you had in your own life? How many of the experiences impacted your life? Finally, which of these experiences changed your life?

In many ways our childhood experiences are smaller, more often unique, yet can have long-term impacts on the ways we collect, examine, and learn from later experiences. Our unique lens of experience creates an individuality as we view the world that is also shaped within the context of the society around us.

As small children, the moon was made of cheese! The adults around us told us so. Of course, at the time, we were easily fooled by adults. Our small experience, lack of data and information, along with an explanation from a knowledgeable person gave us no other information, so in our world the moon was made of cheese. Later, the teen variant of these stories may be explained to require you to seek blinker fluid for your turn signals of your first car. Let's not begin to talk about Santa Claus.

Experiences are simply events where we collect evidence. This evidence is collected through interaction, participation, and observation. We interact, participate, and observe our family and friends as children to create models and theories of our world. As we advance through middle childhood and teenage years, the interactions, observations, and activity participation stretch to include larger segments of our community and society.

Experience is simply data for us to use for our benefit – neither right or wrong, good, or bad. However, as a practical matter, we can classify experiences first-hand (interaction/participation) and second-hand (observation) and in several different modalities (e.g., emotional, mental/intellectual, physical, spiritual, social, simulated). Good experience or bad experience can both be impactful and experienced in one or more modality. We collect building blocks of data/information/evidence to build validity and reliability of our perspective of the world.

Knowledge

Knowledge is best understood from the context of experience. Knowledge is the depth and breadth of information and skills acquired through interaction, participation, observation integrated with an individual's comprehension of connected experiences.

Aristotle delivers an intriguing example explaining the connection between practical knowledge and theoretical knowledge.

> This is why some who do not know, and especially those who have experience, are more practical than others who know; for if a man knew that light meats are digestible and wholesome, but did not know which sorts of meat are light, he would not produce health, but the man who knows that chicken is wholesome is more likely to produce health (Book VI of Nicomachean Ethics).

This quote deserves a bit of explanation. Aristotle is explaining abstract knowledge and practical knowledge. A person that can obtain both book knowledge (second-hand) and practical knowledge (experience) is best. Both forms of knowledge have their weaknesses. A person with theoretical knowledge may know that white meat chicken is wholesome but have no understanding of how to tell the difference between the light and dark. Yet a practical person may know the difference between dark and light, but not know the wholesome advantages. Having knowledge from others combined with the knowledge from your own experiences provide a better overall understanding (knowledge) of a subject.

There is an inextricable connection between knowledge and experience. Experiences in our lives are often overlooked because they were singular or novel events that we don't see, at the time, as impactful in the long-term path of our lives.

A singular event in our life provides us a single data point or single piece of evidence that life happens in a certain way. As we build upon a singular event with more and more similar events, we begin to make connections between the events. Experience is an accumulation of singular events. The connections that we discover between events builds a base of knowledge. Our knowledge is built using our experiences, not because of our experiences.

We gain experience and knowledge as we age, but our key issue is to leverage our experiences to further our knowledge. There is a common myth of the 10,000-hour rule. The premise of this rule is that you will gain expertise through 10,000 hours of repetition and training – about nine years (five days a week, four hours a day). Experience and practice play a role in gaining knowledge and expertise, it is not simply the experience. Not all practice is created equal, not everyone has the same starting place, and not everyone gains the same knowledge from each practice session or experience.

We each gain and connect knowledge at a different rate. When we provide any group of people the same experience (e.g., education, training, etc.), there are significant differences in the impact of that experience on each individual. There are differences in the subjective interpretation of that experience in conjunction with all their other experiences up to that point in their lives. Finally, a person's cognitive ability to understand, classify, and assimilate experience differs individually. The depth and breadth of knowledge we acquire from an experience or set of experiences varies significantly between each person.

Adversity

Merriam-Webster defines adversity as "a state, condition, or instance of serious or continued difficulty or adverse fortune." Synonyms include misfortune, difficulty, distress, disaster, pain, trauma, accident, setback, crisis, catastrophe, tragedy, tough luck, hurting, suffering, and calamity.

However dismal adversity sounds, resilience in the face of adversity makes each of us a better person. Hard things make you a much more interesting person. Adverse circumstances challenge our intellectual ability to overcome. Adversity provides an opportunity for deeper understanding of self. Adversity brings forward the fragility of our existence and allows us to better connect with others encountering adversity in their lives. It often provides humbling experiences, allowing us to better understand how to express compassion, empathy, and kindness to and empathy for others experiencing the same. Overcoming adverse situations is a key component to fostering wisdom in ourselves and others.

We each encounter adversities and adverse misfortunes that shape our lives. Adversity, in and of itself, is not a bad thing. Adversity plays an integral role in fostering wisdom. Each of us, from the earliest memories of our childhood, have experienced adversity and challenge.

This adversity may come in the form of crawling, walking, hitting a baseball ball, a first kiss, a driver's test, navigating the subway, interviewing, or traveling. We have many different common experiences in life, but every life has some experience in adversity. Adversity in our lives has an important role in shaping our belief structure, challenging our multilevel problem-solving skills, strengthening our resolve, and understanding the role of trust. Adversity comes in many forms from the short term and easily overcome (no real problem) to traumatic and life altering. Adversity is the mountains that we climb. What changes is our ability to learn in that environment.

When we encounter adversity in a kind and stable environment, we can learn quickly due to the safe or kind nature of our learning. There are not extenuating circumstances that hinder our ability to learn through interaction, participation, observation, and study. When we encounter adversity in a wicked or hostile environment, we have barriers, hurdles, and instabilities to overcome that will hinder our ability to learn. If we can overcome these hurdles, the learning is hard-earned but rich in both content and context.

From a pure learning perspective, a kind environment can quicken learning. From a wisdom perspective, if we can foster learning also in a wicked, uncertain, chaotic environment we can adapt to learning and growing in both the best and worst conditions.

Trauma is an essential part of being human: These experiences will taint (for better or worse) the remainder of a person's life. Trauma is not sought by anyone; however, it happens to many of us. However, we must seek to overcome these traumas as we would any other adversity. We often hear posttraumatic stress, but seldom do we hear the term posttraumatic growth. Research in posttraumatic growth shows that people are resilient and can grow and become better in the aftermath of trauma. It should be noted that there are adversities, challenges, adverse fortunes, and traumas that are too much for some to overcome without the assistance of trauma professionals and psychotherapy.

Adversity is not an enemy when we are discussing wisdom. Adversity and adverse fortune can either inhibit growth or dynamically enhance individual growth. It's up to us as individuals to leverage our experiences in adversity to master self-awareness, self-learning, and self-reflections. Stories are told of individuals that have overcome adversity to find self-growth. We don't tell the epic stories of the person taking an easy stroll down the lane finding no adversity and no triumph – there is no story to be told. People are better when they do hard things. Adversity, in all sizes, is a necessary step on our pathway to wisdom.

Growth

We grow from where we are planted, and our journey starts there. Everyone has a unique story, a unique childhood, and a unique perspective. Progress is perfection. This is not a race. There is a deliberateness in some individuals to grow their knowledge through interaction, participation, observation, and study. Growing is an outcome of our learning from our knowledge and experience.

Wisdom involves many different traits, but we know that an introspection of self is at the core of that growth. It's not only good enough to have a set of knowledge but to discern patterns of knowledge and experience to understand and overcome novel adverse situations and negative experiences. As we grow with the idea of fostering wisdom, our understanding of ourselves and others grows exponentially with age, knowledge, and experience.

Personal agency becomes a multiplier of growth in wisdom. Personal agency is your personal level of belief that you are responsible for your own feelings, thoughts, and actions, rather than other people controlling your feelings, thoughts, and actions.

Our deliberate efforts to grow ourselves by unlearning old models, building new multilevel models that incorporate personal, community, and societal issues enhances our insights and our ability to see patterns that can be used to solve more complicated issues in the future. Our growth is within a holon of society. We are self-determining independent people creating a course of action while simultaneously existing in larger systems of our communities and society.

If experience and age were highly correlated, we would simply identify *all* our elders as wise. Since we don't identify all our elders as wise, we must deliberately cultivate our personal wisdom rather than waiting for it to be gifted.

> Imagine for a moment that you are currently perfect and existing at this moment of your life.

To grow, we must first assess and accept and appreciate our current circumstances. This perfect existence is a place to grow. Harsh, good. Comfortable, fine. Troubling, this will change. Fostering wisdom is not about getting to a goal or achieving placement in a race. It is about understanding ourselves and others filtered through our knowledge and experience. What is our course of action from our current circumstance?

When we walk a trail for the first time, we view a tree exactly as it is today. We don't know yesterday, and we don't know tomorrow for this tree. We simply see the 100-year-old oak tree in its current state of living. We are making observations today. Different days over a series of years may see three different variations of the tree. Our tree, depending on the time of year, may be mottled. Our tree may have just survived the once in a century storm with limbs splintered and leaves stripped. Our tree may be the model of a perfect oak tree with strong mature limbs casting shade and propagating acorns for its community. But this is only the superficial picture. We know nothing of the heart of the tree, we know nothing of its tannins and internal fortitude.

We still only have a few snapshots of the tree. Its lifetime can span 700 to 1,000 years. The tree is never static, it is always in the process of molecular growth. Its change never stops. Repair, regeneration, reproduction, adapting and interacting happen continuously even though outside observers cannot see the infinitely small changes throughout the tree's lifetime.

Human observation is very similar. We change over time, we are in a constant state of growth, and what we are today is used to shape who we are tomorrow. We are humans with the ability to use our starting point for growth. Our starting point for growth is where we are today. Yesterday shaped us, and we must be willing to live with the yesterday, enjoy the present, and shape the future. Humans can apply insight, experience, and sound judgment. We can develop knowledge, skills, attitudes, and abilities to create a course of action. It's our hope that our decisions for our personal growth led to beneficial and productive decisions.

We are better people when we do hard things. Whether chosen or unchosen, hard things make us more resilient and better able to survive and thrive in a chaotic world. Adversity enriches our ability to grow as we age. Get comfortable being uncomfortable. Learn to adapt and change with today's circumstance to impact future goals.

3 Learning and Unlearning

Searching for Masters

To explore learning, we first must understand how education works. Not from the seat of students but looking at our overall education system to understand why we are trained to learn the way that we do. We are trained to learn. We are encouraged to learn. We are tested on what we learned. Yet, we still have more to learn. Lifelong learning is a truism that cannot be ignored. There is a Zen proverb on learning that is especially useful in understanding how learning and unlearning are critical for our growth and development.

> Once upon a time (yes, all stories start this way), there was a wise Zen master. The people from far and wide saved their money, sacrificed their time, and endured a long and rigorous journey to hear the master's voice and gather a sage understanding of the world. The master shared stories, knowledge, and enlightenment freely in exchange for the individual's free sacrifice in making the journey.
>
> On a particularly cold fall morning, a young scholar finished the long and arduous trip up the high mountain roads and goat trails to visit the master. Though tired, thirsty, and hungry from the seemingly never-ending battles of his travel, he stated a clear goal upon arriving: "I've traveled these many days to ask that you teach me about Zen."
>
> To provide an understanding of his qualifications, the scholars proceed to tell of his life, the schools that he had attended, the renowned teachers that he had learned from, of the theories and ideas harvested, and adventures of the journey, the people he met, the lessons learned and much about a world discovered during his life to this point.

DOI: 10.4324/9781003018759-4

Over the next few days, the teacher worked to teach the student and provide a unique perspective. But each time the teacher tried to explain, the student kept holding on to the teaching of others and holding to his personal notions of the world. Through his experiences the young scholar had constructed an understanding of how the world should be and had difficulty understanding the lessons that the master was trying to teach.

Over the days, the master tried conversation, but was interrupted repeatedly by the adamant scholar who had traveled so far to reach this destination. Seeing that proceeding further was pointless, the master suggested that they take a break and continue lessons over tea near the warmth of a fire. The scholar agreed and they then proceeded inside the master home to sit comfortably at the table in front of the comfortable fire.

Now in the comfort of a warm house, the master poured tea for both. As the warm aromatic tea filled the cup the student watched, looking forward to the warm taste of the tea. The scholar sipped his tea as they sat in contentment. After a few moments the master began to refill the student's cup from the master's own, untouched, cup of tea. As the scholar's cup was filled to the top, the master continued to pour the full cup of tea into the student's cup. The cup, unsurprisingly, overflowed onto the table, onto the floor and then onto the scholar. The scholar jumped in surprise "Stop! The cup is full! Can't you see what you are doing? You should have waited."

The master replied "I know. Your cup is already full of your ideas, impressions, and solutions. You cannot grow until you let go of old ideas and perspectives that already fill you. You have to open yourself and make room for what I have to teach you."

She looked at the young scholar and stated, "If you truly seek to learn, you must first unlearn - you must empty your cup."

The student smiled in silence. The lessons began again with an empty cup and a readiness to grow.

Bruce Lee famously shared, based on this story, "Empty your cup so that it may be filled; become devoid to gain totality." Today, Google processes more than 40,000 searches every second. We gather and consume information because it is so prevalent in our world today. We seek more knowledge to add knowledge to what we already have at our fingertips. We learn more to have more learning. The quest for more data, more information, and more knowledge is overwhelming and endless. In this case, the scholar had plenty of knowledge and information to draw upon.

We are knowledge seekers. We want to know and know more. We are contently full of unorganized information and knowledge, yet we don't know how to distill essence from what we have in front of us. We are asking questions and seeking information and knowledge that will provide the key. We don't quite know what the key does, or which doors it might open. Information and knowledge without meaning is of little use to us in a global knowledge economy.

Classical Education

Classically taught educators in the United State have a style of teaching that has been manipulated and "perfected" in thousands of different ways to reach and teach an ever-changing demographics of students, the spectrum of learning needs, and the variety of individual learning environments. This classical education provides a blueprint for learning that's built with multiple learning contingencies for a generalized student population rather than possessing a lean agility needed in many globally diverse teaching and learning environments. Each elementary and postsecondary teacher is taught the knowledge and skills of becoming a successful teacher. But the complexity of the classroom can be overwhelming. They need to quickly master the multitude of interlinking tools, models, and theories that worked in the laboratory of the teacher preparation institution, but violently meet the shoes-to-the-pavement reality of the classroom. 40–50% of classroom teachers leave teaching within the first five years of their teaching career. This is an unfortunate reality.

While classical education structures can be exceptionally effective within the closed climate of an elementary or secondary classroom, this structure often falls short as we expand to the postsecondary classroom, corporate training environment, or worksite.

For every corporate trainer, there is 0% chance that they had childhood dreams of being a corporate trainer in a company. Trainers in corporations most often move into the profession due to their peer and supervisor observing their mentoring and training of others in their unit, department, or division. Another way to think of this is that the person's peers provided evidentiary support of the person's ability to become a trainer. Entry into the profession can be gained through a higher education degree, but most often trainers are hired from within the corporate population, then receive professional training.

Trainers enter their field with an aptitude to train, but often have limited knowledge and skills in learning theory and learning frameworks. The trainer has the same needs as any other educator and has many classroom management problems that are very different from the teacher in an elementary and secondary classroom.

Throughout the remaining sections, you will find trainer and teacher used interchangeably for the most part. Education is process oriented, while training is outcome oriented. There are several instances where the professions of teaching and training are different, but typically these differences are only within the context of the subject taught, age of the learner, and organizational identification. There are certainly differences between adults and children and even more so when you explore the youngest-young and oldest-old populations, but the differences can largely be described as outliers. For a moment, ignore the semantics and the subject of human learning will start to make sense. The outliers will be addressed as we go along.

On Teaching

The art and science of teaching is an endless multidisciplinary field that requires a dueling demands of subject-matter expertise and professional teaching skills update. There's a large body of literature describing both pedagogy (the way kids learn) and andragogy (the way adults learn). These categories inherently created context for us to divide the way that we teach each of these groups. Pedagogy is a child-focused teaching theory describing children as extrinsically motivated that are dependent on the teacher for guidance, knowledge, and evaluation. Andragogy is an adult-focused teaching theory describing adults as intrinsically motivated to gain experience and solve problems.

Native-internet-learners and native-mobile-learners have quickly disproven much of what we thought we knew about the learning differences between kids and adults. In today's global knowledge economy, our classical learning theories tend to be less than trustworthy. Whether child or adult, we are uniquely the same in our desire for personal agency in learning.

When we are taught, we need to:

* Understand why the subject is important to us, individually.
  Why is this content knowledge important? Learners connect through a teacher/trainer/mentor's personal understanding of why the subject is important (as a motivator/witness/storyteller). As a learner, this is our external motivation to learn the content.
* Learn the content and context of the subject matter.

What's to be known? Learners need a basic roadmap to the solution, or a standard course of action that can be used to investigate and solve problems. We rely on the expertise of the teacher/trainer/mentor and their ability to communicate the knowledge. This provides the learner an opportunity to understand procedures modeled correctly. As a learner, this is our roadmap for solving future problems.

- Practice what has been taught – it is very difficult to understand complex or hands-on topics without the ability to "try"; and

    Practice. Learners need the opportunity to practice solving and attempting to solve problems using roadmaps and standard courses of action taught. We rely on the teacher/trainer/mentor to present scenarios, problems, case studies, and unique situations that allow us to work in a safe environment and learn productively while the teacher provides skilled mentoring and oversight.

- To explore, experiment, question, and ponder the content delivered by the teacher/trainer/mentor.

    Explore! Learners need the space and opportunity to think, explore, succeed, and fail. Learners need to teach themselves. Learners can use their insight and intuition and their experience in conjunction with their new knowledge, skills, attitudes, and abilities to explore a beneficial course of action. Learners learn resilience in self-discovery rather than reliance on the teacher/trainer/mentor while exploring the newly taught materials.

Is this dependent on a person's chronological age? NO. Simply, we must consider that learners are learners, regardless of age. Learners can be self-directed and seek guidance to learn more effectively. Learners want control over their learning experience. Teachers/trainers are responsible for planning and teaching the knowledge, skills, attitudes, and abilities to succeed in the subject area and evaluating their teaching effectiveness. Learners are equally responsible for how much they learn (intrinsic motivation) and are responsible for both planning and evaluating their own learning. As we move from children to adults, we are granted much more self-agency and must learn to control our own learning. Our classroom becomes the world.

Growing in Kind Environments and Wicked Environments

Contextual learning is a methodology designed to help learners apply new abilities to real-life experiences. Learners can best understand the meaning and application of theories and processes when it is presented in the context of real-world problems and solutions. Information must be accessible for knowledge sharing. This contextualization of learning provides a clear and effective path to achievement of learning goals. More importantly, it allows the learner to better convert information to knowledge. This transfer is at the heart of learning and performance innovation. Within the context of learning, we are in a constant state of gathering experiences and often, hopefully, learning from those experiences.

There is a warning here: In contrast to what is commonly believed about learning, our growth can be enhanced, or hampered, by new learning. We are the caretakers of what we learn and how we integrate that learning into our previous knowledge and experience. While we leave this responsibility to the teachers in children, adults become accountable for their lifelong learning and unlearning.

Teaching and learning are often relegated to the classroom; however, outside the classroom we are inundated with information, knowledge, and new learning experiences every day. Some of these learning experiences are structured with rapid and reliable feedback, while other learning experiences have hidden or incorrect information or feedback that is confusing, conflicting, delayed, infrequent, nonexistent, or inaccurate. This poor feedback often reinforces the wrong type of behavior. Research describes two major types of environments where we learn: Kind and Wicked.

Kind environments

Kind environments are few in adult life, but when we find them, we must take advantage of the rapid learning opportunity that they provide to us. While the term "kind" environment isn't commonly used in our everyday lexicon, we have experienced it. We find kinder environments in the classroom and in our games. Kind environments are comforting and reassuring but are not necessarily easy.

Kind environments have recurring patterns that we can learn to follow. All practical and appropriate information is available to the person in the environment, and the information is totally reliable and readily available to the person when it's needed. Kind environments are structured. A person can see clear correlations between decision-making behaviors and outcomes. In these environments, a person can see improvements through repetitive practice by utilizing a clear set of rules in a confined and controlled environment. Finally, kind environments reinforce correct behavior that will lead to success.

Here are a few examples of kind environments that most of us have encountered: Chess, golf, bowling, and most school homework. While none of these would be ranked easy by any measure, they meet all of the qualifications of kind environments – targets of learning and performance are very clear. Remember, kind does not mean easy.

Video games are another great example. As my sons are often telling me: "That boss is easy, once you learn the patterns."

My sons have observed me beginning the same "boss fights" again, and again, and again. But, as in any type of kind environment/problem, the boss fight is in a contained area, there are recurring patterns to the stabs, swipes, and kicks and the feedback is reliable (I die when I do it wrong). Keep in mind the feedback loop is meaningful, clear, and immediate – good decisions are rewarded and poor strategies and tactics lead to defeat.

The clear upside of kind environmental learning is that guidance and practice can lead to success. Within the kind environment, specialized expertise with reasoned decision-making is more important than generalist knowledge since specialized knowledge of processes, feedback, and results is important. Learning environments vary greatly, and kind environments are at one end of the spectrum. At the other end of the spectrum is the wicked learning environment.

Wicked environments

On the opposite end of the spectrum from our kind environment is a wicked environment. Wicked learning environments can be described as having hidden or incorrect information, or with feedback that is confusing, conflicting, delayed, infrequent, nonexistent, and inaccurate. This feedback often reinforces the wrong type of behavior.

The stock market is a great example of a wicked environment. The stock market has many variables that impact the increase or decline in a single stock's price. Increasing demand, decreasing supply, corporate earnings, valuation, future earnings projections, growth rates, leveraging, perceived risk, inflation, strength of market, trends, liquidity, world events, and many other variables individually or in combination can create growth or decreasing demand in a stock that affects its market price. Unlike our kind environments, volatility, interpretation, and a fuzzy crystal ball create a vicious learning curve for both the novices and experts. The same can be said of fields such as medicine or law.

In chaotic or complex environments, experts don't always perform better than others. Sometimes these unclear environments can lead to a discrepancy between what is being observed or happening in the environment and the truth of what is happening. This distorts information and leads to poor decision-making. While growing levels of expertise does improve deductive and inductive reasoning ability, it does not always lead to superior performance by experts vs. novices. More specifically, within the wicked learning environment, generalized expertise (for reasoned decision-making) is more important than specialized knowledge. The complex and chaotic learning environments require a much wider range of knowledge (breadth) rather than a specific (depth) of knowledge to adapt to changing feedback and judging truthfulness of feedback for decision-making. Learning environments vary greatly and are set at the other end of the spectrum from kind environments.

What doesn't kill you makes you stronger is a phrase that represents many wicked learning environments. There are clear upsides of kind learning environments in that guidance and practice can lead to success, but there are also clear advantages to learning in a harsh wicked environment. We often, in real life, don't have our choice of learning environments.

Thriving

· *We can't teach people not to fear - we can teach people to be brave.*

Kind and wicked environments are at different ends of the spectrum. There's a lot of room in between to have a mixture of the two types of environments. We can classify something as wicked or kind but there are different degrees of kind or wicked learning environments (Figure 3.1).

Kind and wicked environments expose us to many different challenges that can aid in our path to wisdom. The greatest changes in our lives happen at the very edge of our comfort zones. Humans are uniquely positioned to learn in many ways and in almost *every* environment. This learning can be progressive or digressive. The adage that we are a product of our environment holds true for everyone.

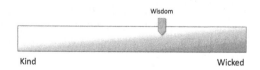

Figure 3.1 Kind/wicked spectrum.

The classroom or training room is the easiest place to talk about a learning environment because it is easiest to visualize. As adult learners, we need to recognize and assess the learning environment. Notice that the responsibility is placed on the adult learner, not the teacher or trainer. The classroom, in most cases, leans toward a kind environment rather than wicked.

Take for example, classroom flight training:

> The pilot training classroom is a relatively kind learning environment. The textbook, classroom training, assignment and classrooms are bound by the walls of the classroom.
>
> Compare this to pre-flight simulator training. Instructors now have added controls that can be changed to send the student into virtual rain and nasty updrafts and cross winds. The student-pilots instruments can be manipulated to provide feedback to the pilot. At one moment the pilot may receive reliable instrument reading that can be used to make in flight correction. At other moments conflict and incorrect instrument feedback is provided to the pilot to train multi-level problem solving, flexibility, self-control and trust while building competent personal agency and responsibility. However, on our spectrum from kind to wicked, we are in a less kind learning environment. Pilots are trained to make sound judgements and chart a course of action that will keep their aircraft and all souls aboard alive in a worst-case scenario.
>
> Can it be more wicked? Now consider the learning environment when mother nature is manipulating a disaster. Learning in the real world with mother nature as the manipulator:
>
> When flying an aircraft, 99.99% of the time your airspeed indicator and vertical speed indicator (how quickly you are climbing in feet per minute) are accurate creating a relatively a kind environment – what you expect to happen, happens. However, there is a wicked situation that can happen where these indications are deceitful. A microburst occasionally happens. What does this look like? Fill your sink with water and point a blower dryer straight down at the water from a foot or two above. The air rushes downward (downdraft) until it reaches the water. Once it can't move down anymore, it will move out and up again (outflow). When this happens in real world weather, the downdraft can be moving at speeds of over 100 miles an hour.
>
> When a plane is coming into land and is near the ground, it slows down, and landing gear is deployed. As the aircraft reaches the invisible outflow of air current it is pushed upward, and the

airspeed increases with the push. While the instrumentation is providing accurate momentary information, it isn't showing the whole picture. Gauges indicate that the aircraft is now over performing since the plane is now high on altitude and high on-air speed – the pilot must quickly correct. The pilot pulls the power to decrease airspeed and nose the aircraft down to descend to the correct approach.

Now the wicked. Just as the pilot begins to stabilize the aircraft back on approach with a lower power setting, they will cross from the outflow to the powerful downflow. The downdraft forces the plane down aggressively. The pilot must react quickly to try to outperform the invisible downdraft. However, the pilot is at a severe disadvantage as they have decreased power and spool up time which, in a jet aircraft, can range from a second or two to over 15 seconds. Depending on the aircraft's altitude from the ground and airspeed, it could be unrecoverable. From the initial indication of the aircraft over performing to being in the dirt could easily be less than 20 seconds. A pilot's experience, awareness, intuition, and training prepare them to make sound judgements and chart a course of action that will keep their aircraft and all souls aboard alive in a worst-case scenario.

The idea of wicked and kind learning environments can help us understand the process of learning and how to foster wisdom in every aspect of our lives. Does it matter whether I'm a specialist or a generalist? It depends, we know from the academic research that specialists are better equipped to thrive in kind environments, while generalists are better equipped to thrive in wicked environments. At the end of the day we must learn, through experience, to both survive and thrive in many different environments, utilizing different strategies for understanding both environments. We don't have control of where we are learning, but there is always an opportunity to learn and grow wiser.

Our learning environments, whether wicked or kind, provide us an opportunity to grow our own learning and, therefore, our wisdom through adverse situations that challenge our current model of the world. With any learning experience we have to also ask: "Is this true? When does this happen? When does this work? When does it not work?"

Our global knowledge economy is growing and changing at an exponential rate. We cannot hold firm to ideas of the past. We must ask ourselves if past belief structures will still apply to the future. We must become comfortable with change and develop the ability to distinguish between the reality of our world today, and what we observed in the past. The truth of today may not apply to tomorrow.

Unlearning

The Greek philosopher Antisthenes stated, "the most useful piece of learning for the uses of life is to unlearn what is not true." This statement is likely more useful now than it was at the end of 400 BC. The need for rapid learning, and therefore unlearning, is exponentially larger in our modern and global information economy. As children, we are provided with evidence and trusted individuals (e.g., parents, friends, and teachers). We lend them cognitive authority to guide our understanding due to our own lack of concrete knowledge and experience. We are instructed in the truths and learn from our mentors to build our mental models of our world. In previous academic writing, my team and I have described unlearning as:

> Not as forgetting, but rather as the process of selecting models and paradigms that improve outdated ones. These improved models and methods can then better match the changing workplace demographics and provide opportunities to engage the workforce and foster wisdom through appropriate policies, practices, and norms.

Unlearning is utilized by the skilled learners to grow beyond their previous education and training. The process of unlearning needs to be understood and implemented daily. The amount of information that we receive each day is extraordinary. The process of unlearning is not taught in classical education; rather we build and warehouse data, information, and knowledge. There's a desire to collect even at the risk of losing connected meaning in archived catalog of gathered information.

Unlearning isn't the same as forgetting. Forgetting is better described, for our purposes, as accidental unlearning. Unlearning is weighing, judging, comparing, discerning, and deciding if a new model or paradigm should replace outdated ones. It doesn't mean that there's an expiration date on every model or idea, but it does require that we reassess what we know to be true.

Bruce Lee, in *Wisdom for the Wise*, simplifies this point: "Absorb what is useful, discard what is useless and add what is specifically your own." The idea of unlearning provides individuals tremendous flexibility in the way that we think about the learning process. Our understanding cannot be static.

Why Unlearn?

Let's look at wisdom, for a moment, as mosaic or stained glass window:

Step 1: Reflection. Consider each tile of your previous knowledge and experience as a mosaic windowpane of your life – all the experiences, all the knowledge, all of the information gathered and processed, all of the understanding.

This constructed window is akin to our lens through which we look at every new life experience. It becomes our "lens of truth." Our initial reaction to future experiences is impacted directly by our past experiences. Visualize your mosaic window. Reflect and imagine what that mosaic looks like right now – today.

Step 2: Deconstruction. Visualize each of those large and small experiences (tiles) laying on the workbench. There are a lot of pieces. If you look through each individual tile, you'll see a different image of the world you are seeing. This is much the same way as we view the world through our experiences. Some panes may be transparent, clouded, colored, colorful, tainted, cracked, or completely opaque. These tiles of experience, knowledge, and understanding tint our view of our world. An easy or hard childhood, trauma, rich experiences, travel, relationships, objectivity, belief structures, insight, and intuition all color the mosaic of tiles that we must work with to construct our window.

Our relationships with others serve as reflection on our own understanding of self. We better understand our emotions, feelings, thoughts, and behaviors through our interaction with the world around us. We master personal agency to build responsibility for our thoughts, feelings, and actions. Our resilience in adversity and self-challenge experience may be insightful, painful, joyful, or restricting. We build sound judgment by making bad and good choices. The consequences of these choices are tiles to be used.

Step 3: Assessment: Some of these thousand tiles are important and anchoring points in our lives. Whether good or bad, they are a large part of how we identify ourselves. Some of these tiles are leftover and no longer useful to move our life forward – they reside as simple experiences to be catalogued and warehoused. The remaining pieces round out our understanding of ourselves and others.

Step 4: Cheat: This is your mosaic window, and it can be created in any way that you desire. Become your own magician. Start creating a mosaic for yourself. Move back to a thousand pieces on the workbench and start reconstructing. Use the key pieces. They build our belief structures, integrity, responsibility, trust, judgments, perception, and perseverance. What if one or more of the key experiences are negative and build doubt, distrust, and fear? Throw them out? Maybe. Remember, you are your own magician, change, and morph it.

It was an experience in adversity that you survived. What did it teach you not to do? How are you stronger and more resilient? What perspective did it provide you? Hard experiences are a lesson in adversity. You are your magician, and you must create the change. A positive, growth attitude to adversity will not erase the adversity. It will allow us to focus on a positive course of action. Setbacks, adversity, and challenge can be morphed to positive. Your mosaic will be unique. It will remain unfinished and uniquely changeable.

We don't have the choice of many of our experiences or lessons taught. It is our choice, as an adult, how we interpret and use this knowledge. We are taught views of the world that are not correct – they have been proven to be incorrect. For many, it's easier to be wrong and hang on to a wrong belief rather than admit they are wrong. Examine each tile, determine whether it's needed, whether it's still relevant, and how it interconnects with each of the other pieces that we've collected over a lifetime of knowledge and earned experience. Unlearning isn't forgetting what was but utilizing only those tiles that move us forward.

Learn, unlearn, evolve, and repeat.

4   Pathways of Wisdom

We don't have the same starting line in life. There's no way to explain away the fact that some people start with more advantages than others in this world. The starting line for education and success are not the same for all. We can't choose our parents and the decisions that they made for us before we were old enough to have personal agency. For parents, graduating from high school, learning a trade, attending college, having a solid career, living a healthy lifestyle, and creating a stable home all provide a better chance for their children's success. A person's negative early childhood experience and socioeconomic disadvantages make a difference. However, if they are overcome and leveraged, these early adversities are steppingstones toward wisdom. Every person has problems that may or may not be their fault, but at some point, it's up to that person to leverage their problems to evolve and thrive. We must critically evaluate, forgive where appropriate, solve, and chart a course forward. Life is not a "kind" learning environment and is very wicked for some. We learn the flexibility to overcome and thrive in any situation.

All too often, we negate and suppress the adversities and challenges that were put in our path. Consider for a moment someone without any adversity or challenges. A person without any adversity or challenge has little opportunity to earn experience in a harsh/challenging/wicked environment; they have little opportunity to develop a resilience to difficulty. From the perspective of wisdom, a person with little experience in adversity or challenge is at a disadvantage to those who lived, learned, evolved, and thrived.

This is not to diminish the destructive and crippling effects of trauma and the real possibility of posttraumatic stress of individuals. Posttraumatic growth is a viable path from trauma. Overwhelming adverse or trauma experiences may require professional assistance. We need the help of mentoring partners, family, friends, and professionals to

DOI: 10.4324/9781003018759-5

understand the intimate relationship between traumatic experiences and current emotions, thoughts, feelings, and behaviors. Just as we get a helping hand on a difficult trail, we also need a hand to understand and overcome obstacles in our lives. We are alive and there is a path forward.

Charting a Path

The pinnacle of human performance is wisdom. Our path to this pinnacle will include success, setbacks, and failure. Yes, at times we will become lost. If we are going to climb a mountain, we will find smooth parts of the trail. These parts will be smooth sailing for us. We will encounter barriers, switchbacks, decision points, dead ends, blisters, thirst, and fatigue. If you find that the last part of the climb is the steepest and most challenging, it will push your knowledge, skills, experience, and understanding of yourself. This is truly the hardest and most satisfying part of the journey.

Try the following short exercise on taking a journey:

> *Take out a map of the United States and consider it carefully. Located two cities on opposite sides (e.g., Los Angeles and New York, Seattle and Miami, Laredo, and Detroit). You are welcome to substitute any two distant global cities.*

Now that you've chosen your starting point, plot the travel to the other city. How will you travel? This is where the decision gets a little more complicated. We can travel by plane, train, or automobile. Maybe even a motorcycle, motorhome, bike, or by the soles of your shoes. How about a combination of any or all of the above?

What is the goal? If our goal is speed, we can begin to plot the fastest and most efficient travel between the two destinations. Making the best time is the most popular choice made by many people every day. Why? It's direct, efficient, and a standard of expected practice.

Careers are often plotted in this manner. You find the most efficient path to achieving a beginning to begin your career through education, training, and/or certification. Our education and training provide much of the knowledge and experience that we need to be productive employees. We accumulate data and information, learn systematic thinking, problem-solving, organization, categorizations, calculation, contextualization, synthesis, competence, and assemble tacit and explicit knowledge. Additionally, we begin to understand the context of relationships between data, information, and knowledge, build our belief structures, and develop drive, perseverance, and personal agency. Finally, we evolve our understanding through interactions to develop trust, sharing, integrity, and accountability, to name a few.

Choosing the destination is important. For many, the destination (goal) is knowledge and success. When this is the goal, adversity becomes a barrier to a learning and growth process. It's little wonder that adversity is looked at in such a negative light. As we "fly over" with only a singular success in mind we gain little diversity of experience. There becomes a point where every airplane trip feels the same and cities morph to a singular description. A train trip, car/motorcycle, bike, or feet each provide a better tapestry of experience as we travel because we have more time to explore and interact. Yet, sadly, we most often go back to the plane that flies us over a rich culture to reach our success goals.

What if we reassess the goal? What if we begin to chart a different path between the two cities? Consider a different way to get to the destination. Every mode of transportation has both its intrinsic and extrinsic advantages and disadvantages. Rather than plot the traditional route, we choose another. This time we chart an avenue to our destination with rich depth and expansive breadth experiences. This new path will require more planning, more patience, more time, more care, more communication, and more attention to our surroundings. Taking the time to explore leads to a richer experience. We are enriched by different experiences and should be emboldened to explore, learn from our mistakes, and open avenues for knowledge discovery.

Charting a path for personal wisdom parallels this exercise. Much of the time, our decisions are made based on accepted practice. We do what we are told is right or what we believe to be acceptable. Our goals are predicated on what is socially acceptable. We most often choose the accepted and well-traveled path. For most people, education, family, and career are the right path. It's easy to replicate; everyone is taking that path. Our personal pathway to wisdom is ours to create. It's the narrow, less traveled, path that diverts slightly from the other path, but that small deviation can have a great consequence in where we arrive.

Beginning from Here

If we created a panel of 50 different wisdom experts from around the world and asked each to define and explain wisdom in a few sentences, we would have 50 different definitions and explanations of wisdom. Our personal experiences of interacting with the wise people in our personal lives form a working definition of wisdom that help us better understand the concept. We have been taught that old and wise can be synonymous, but we know many older family, friends, and colleagues. Yet, inherently discriminate between those who are intelligent, kind, helpful, and wise. Our first understanding of the wise comes first from our personal interaction with people that we personally believe to be wise.

How to become wise is all too often answered: Gain experience and grow old. This can't be the right answer.

Everyone gains experience as they grow older simply from the act of experience but learning from experience is our goal. Experience is gained, and accumulated, through our direct participation and observation of real events that affect our emotions, feelings, thoughts, and behaviors. While we certainly learn from other's experiences, experiential learning is best because it is wrapped in the context of our personal lived experiences. Age is actively happening to all of us. If gaining experience and growing old was the most appropriate way to grow wise, we would be surrounded by the old and wise.

It's difficult to move forward if we don't know first where we are and second knowing where we want to be. Our characteristics of the wise are divided into three categories: *Knowledge and Experience, Understanding of Self*, and *Understanding of Others*. Each of these areas provides an important set of characteristics that are leveraged for personal growth (Figure 4.1).

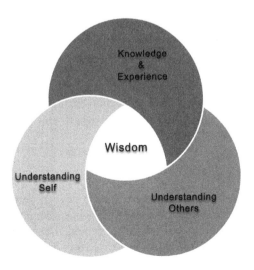

Figure 4.1 Wisdom constructs.

Personal growth is a process of moving forward in incremental steps from who we are today (an honest assessment of self) to a pinnacle of who we will be in the future. Personal growth is not happenstance. Personal growth cannot be taken for granted as an assumption that we will be a better version of ourselves in the future. It's just as likely that without care and thoughtfulness that we will begin to decline. We must practice nurturing and caring for our personal growth.

The remainder of this chapter discusses self-assessment, reflection, and planning. The focus is to provide a workbook that provides each person an opportunity for reflection and personalization. We each understand and describe wise in a very different manner, and we aren't wrong. Wisdom is a subject that isn't a science and starts with context of understanding. Our best understanding of wise is our personal experience with the wise people in our life and with our knowledge of notable wise people.

Wise is much more rare than knowledgeable. We value and treasure those who we personally consider wise. What makes them different, and how can we model their traits and characteristics to better build our personal capability? Our world needs more wisdom. Our world needs more wise individuals.

There is tremendous literature on leadership that can provide insight on wise decision-making. We can learn a lot about wise decision-making from leadership literature. As a starting point, servant leadership and primal leadership may most closely parallel how the wise operate as leaders. Not all leaders are wise, and not all wise are leaders. Sadly, supervisors, managers, and other organizational leaders seldom are listed in our personal list of wise people. Leaders are most often seen as knowledgeable and experienced, but the personal and interpersonal traits are sometimes lacking. Do we need more wise leaders? Yes. Wise people certainly can be formal or informal leaders in our different organizations. If leveraged, these individuals bring tremendous value to both the organization's bottom line and overall culture.

Let's get started with assessment.

Knowledge and Experience

We need to first understand where we are now to better understand our areas of exceeding success and areas that we can improve. Some of the characteristics in the assessment provided may be unfamiliar -- that's ok. We are on a journey of self-discovery and self-improvement. This a formative evaluation, it simply serves as a snapshot – more accurately, a retrospective assessment looking back five years to better assess our growth.

Knowledge and Experience
This is a set of paired questions to understand your personal growth in each characteristic.
Assess your personal knowledge, skills, attitudes, or abilities in each of the areas.

Abstract reasoning	Poor	Fair	Good	Fair	Excellent
Past	O	O	O	O	O
Now	O	O	O	O	O
Competent	Poor	Fair	Good	Fair	Excellent
Past	O	O	O	O	O
Now	O	O	O	O	O
Explicit knowledge	Poor	Fair	Good	Fair	Excellent
Past	O	O	O	O	O
Now	O	O	O	O	O
Implicit knowledge	Poor	Fair	Good	Fair	Excellent
Past	O	O	O	O	O
Now	O	O	O	O	O
Insightful	Poor	Fair	Good	Fair	Excellent
Past	O	O	O	O	O
Now	O	O	O	O	O
Intuition	Poor	Fair	Good	Fair	Excellent
Past	O	O	O	O	O
Now	O	O	O	O	O
Learner	Poor	Fair	Good	Fair	Excellent
Past	O	O	O	O	O
Now	O	O	O	O	O
Objective	Poor	Fair	Good	Fair	Excellent
Past	O	O	O	O	O
Now	O	O	O	O	O
Perceptive	Poor	Fair	Good	Fair	Excellent
Past	O	O	O	O	O
Now	O	O	O	O	O
Sound judgment	Poor	Fair	Good	Fair	Excellent
Past	O	O	O	O	O
Now	O	O	O	O	O
Systematic thinking	Poor	Fair	Good	Fair	Excellent
Past	O	O	O	O	O
Now	O	O	O	O	O
Unlearning	Poor	Fair	Good	Fair	Excellent
Past	O	O	O	O	O
Now	O	O	O	O	O

Knowledge and Experience describe a wide range of characteristics that allow an individual to grow their personal depth and breadth of knowledge and experience. Many of these characteristics could also describe individuals who are intelligent and well informed (e.g., competence, learning, explicit and implicit/tacit knowledge). There are other characteristics that may not immediately come to the forefront in discussion on knowledge, including insight, intuition, and sound judgment. Intuition and insight are two characteristics that are ignored in our education systems and training programs, but they are both often mentioned in the discussion of wisdom.

Intuition is the ability to make decisions (yes/no) without conscious cognitive reasoning or deliberation. This is often referred to as a gut feeling that comes from previous cumulative experiences and knowledge. These are our in-the-moment judgments that come from unconscious pattern recognition, perception, and instinctive understanding.

Insight is understanding of a non-obvious situation or problem by utilizing personal experiences combined with systems understanding and analysis. Insight is closely tied to implicit/tacit knowledge and provides individuals the ability to reflect, assess and overcome barriers to understanding, learning, and communicating. This decision making is based on deep knowledge and a depth and breadth of experience. Insight and intuition are developed through integration of many different experiences, understanding of processes, principles and how those principles are applied to future situations. Personal wisdom is amplified by knowledge acquisition and assimilation and applied to new situations through personal values, beliefs, and understanding. Wisdom increases our effectiveness and efficiency.

Sound judgment is our capability and capacity to objectively draw conclusions based on facts, circumstance, gained knowledge and experience, risk analysis, abstract reasoning, intuition, and systematic thinking. Sound judgment is learned through experiences making both good and bad judgments. Sound judgment is the best judgment for the conditions or circumstances, calculated risk, and prediction of a successful outcome.

In Consilience: The Unity of Knowledge, E.O. Wilson states: "We are drowning in information, while starving for wisdom. The world henceforth will be run by synthesizers, people able to put together the right information at the right time, think critically about it, and make important choices wisely" (1993, p. 294). All too often we are awarded for productivity rather than sound judgment and wisdom. It's of little wonder why we seek productivity rather than wisdom. We should be striving to become not only knowledge seekers, but ultimately to work toward wisdom.

Consider your list of the wise, again. An often-mentioned characteristic of the wise is the ability to hear, consider, and understand our situation and see a viable path forward. Our wise mentors may have never been in the situation that's being related through our story, but they draw on a seemingly endless depth and breadth of knowledge and experience to find a solution. They think in the abstract, distilling the essence of the situation to foster a beneficial course of action that we can use to move forward.

Understanding of Others

We need to first understand where we are now to better understand our areas of exceeding success and areas that we can improve. The formative evaluation below serves as a snapshot or, more accurately, a retrospective assessment looking back five years to better assess our growth. The second assessment is introspective to understand our personal growth.

Understanding Others
This is a set of paired questions to understand your personal growth in each characteristic.
Assess your personal knowledge, skills, attitudes, or abilities in each of the areas.

Accountability	Poor	Fair	Good	Fair	Excellent
Past	O	O	O	O	O
Now	O	O	O	O	O
Benevolent	Poor	Fair	Good	Fair	Excellent
Past	O	O	O	O	O
Now	O	O	O	O	O
Compassionate	Poor	Fair	Good	Fair	Excellent
Past	O	O	O	O	O
Now	O	O	O	O	O
Empathetic	Poor	Fair	Good	Fair	Excellent
Past	O	O	O	O	O
Now	O	O	O	O	O
Ethical	Poor	Fair	Good	Fair	Excellent
Past	O	O	O	O	O
Now	O	O	O	O	O
Generous	Poor	Fair	Good	Fair	Excellent
Past	O	O	O	O	O
Now	O	O	O	O	O
Influential	Poor	Fair	Good	Fair	Excellent
Past	O	O	O	O	O
Now	O	O	O	O	O
Inspiring	Poor	Fair	Good	Fair	Excellent
Past	O	O	O	O	O
Now	O	O	O	O	O
Listener	Poor	Fair	Good	Fair	Excellent
Past	O	O	O	O	O
Now	O	O	O	O	O
Responsible	Poor	Fair	Good	Fair	Excellent
Past	O	O	O	O	O
Now	O	O	O	O	O
Sacrificing	Poor	Fair	Good	Fair	Excellent
Past	O	O	O	O	O
Now	O	O	O	O	O
Sharing	Poor	Fair	Good	Fair	Excellent
Past	O	O	O	O	O
Now	O	O	O	O	O

Understanding of Others allows an individual to grow their personal depth and breadth of understanding of other people. The field of emotional intelligence, as we know it today, was led by Howard Gardner's 1983 book titled *Frames of Mind: The Theory of Multiple Intelligences* with the premise that traditional intelligence (e.g., IQ) didn't provide a full picture of a person's cognitive intelligence. He argued that intelligence included interpersonal intelligence and intrapersonal intelligence. Garner's premise was expanded and popularized with Daniel Goleman's publication of *Emotional Intelligence: Why It Can Matter More Than IQ*. Goleman's work in emotional intelligence later led to the publication of primal leadership to help leaders understand how to lead better.

Our perception of the wise is built through our interaction with the people around us that we, personally, consider to be wise. It's their ability to relate to others. Often, in discussing wisdom, the wise are described by their ability to inspire others, situational influence, honesty in communication, and a deep code of ethics, providing profound interpersonal sharing and trust.

Our favorite and most impactful teachers are often mentioned as being wise. This is often due to a combination of pedagogy (the way they teach) and their powerful and unique personalities. While all teachers/trainers can provide expertise in their subject area, a smaller number of teachers understand students and develop a rich learning environment with trusting interactions. The wise in our lives listen with benevolence and compassion, share with generosity and humbleness, and advise honestly. It's little wonder that our wise pass their knowledge to us to foster wisdom in others.

Understanding of Self

We need to first understand where we are now to better understand our areas of exceeding success and areas that we can improve. The formative evaluation below serves as a snapshot – or more accurately, a retrospective assessment in looking back five years to better assess our growth. The third assessment is introspective to understand our personal growth in understanding our personal ability.

Understanding Self

This is a set of paired questions to understand your personal growth in each characteristic.

Assess your personal knowledge, skills, attitudes, or abilities in each of the areas.

Agency	Poor	Fair	Good	Fair	Excellent
Past	O	O	O	O	O
Now	O	O	O	O	O

Belief system	Poor	Fair	Good	Fair	Excellent
Past	O	O	O	O	O
Now	O	O	O	O	O
Courageous	Poor	Fair	Good	Fair	Excellent
Past	O	O	O	O	O
Now	O	O	O	O	O
Driven	Poor	Fair	Good	Fair	Excellent
Past	O	O	O	O	O
Now	O	O	O	O	O
Flexible	Poor	Fair	Good	Fair	Excellent
Past	O	O	O	O	O
Now	O	O	O	O	O
Mindful	Poor	Fair	Good	Fair	Excellent
Past	O	O	O	O	O
Now	O	O	O	O	O
Optimistic	Poor	Fair	Good	Fair	Excellent
Past	O	O	O	O	O
Now	O	O	O	O	O
Patient	Poor	Fair	Good	Fair	Excellent
Past	O	O	O	O	O
Now	O	O	O	O	O
Perseverant	Poor	Fair	Good	Fair	Excellent
Past	O	O	O	O	O
Now	O	O	O	O	O
Self-directed	Poor	Fair	Good	Fair	Excellent
Past	O	O	O	O	O
Now	O	O	O	O	O
Self-growth	Poor	Fair	Good	Fair	Excellent
Past	O	O	O	O	O
Now	O	O	O	O	O
Self-reliant	Poor	Fair	Good	Fair	Excellent
Past	O	O	O	O	O
Now	O	O	O	O	O

These characteristics allow us to grow our depth and breadth of understanding to master our emotions, feelings, thoughts, and behaviors. Self-mastery is the foundation that allows the wise to reach to help others. This does not mean perfect. This doesn't mean without flaw.

However much we desire to control our destiny, there's actually very little that we perceive that we can control without the influence of other people. Yet, the list is large enough that we can have influence on our own life. We control, in respect to ourselves and others, accountability, behaviors, effort, energy investments, expression, fitness, forgiveness, friendships, gratitude, happiness, honesty, kindness, love, personal ethics, resilience, respect, response to adversity, self-talk, and thoughts.

These are actions that we can directly impact and do something about. This list is intended to provide context to the following: I only control myself. The mastery of self is distinct in the wise and is valued by those who seek them. As we seek a path to wisdom, mastering self is an excellent starting point. Why? This is a singular aspect of our lives that we alone control. Maya Angelou wisely states, "You may not control all the events that happen to you, but you can decide not to be reduced by them."

Self-efficacy reflects our personal confidence in the ability to exert control over our motivation, behavior, and social environment. Self-awareness, self-control, self-direction, self-learning, self-reliance, and self-reflection together provide us the psychological tools that we need to build our self-efficacy to take control and accountability for our own learning and growth.

Just as a plant needs energy to grow, so do people. We manage the ebbs and flows of our energy to manage our growth and productivity. Nothing is free. Our health, relationships, jobs, education, community, and environment will energize or drain our energy, and, therefore, our ability to grow and be productive. In their book, *The Power of Full Engagement*, Loehr and Schwartz (2003) describe four types of energy that interact with one another: Physical, emotional, mental, and spiritual. They emphasize that "because energy capacity diminishes both with overuse and with underuse, we must balance energy expenditure with intermittent energy renewal" (p. 11). Our physical energy includes physical fitness, nutrition, and recovery. Successful management of physical energy leads to increased productivity. Our emotional energy impacts our feelings, thoughts, and behaviors. Successful management is closely aligned with self-efficacy and provides us self-governance, confidence, purposefulness, and growth. Mental energy is our attention and focus. Learning skills and knowledge can consume mental energy, but it can also energize us through innovative thought and new direction. Spiritual energy is how we discover a sense of meaning and purpose. Spiritual energy is working on our happiness, contentment, self-talk, thoughts, feelings, and overall peace. Energy can be gained or lost with use. The management of our energy is even more important than time management. Engaging time to reenergize through a quick run, yoga, a nap, meditation is an investment in ourselves. Engaging time with the important people in our lives that help us grow and reenergize. At the other end of the spectrum, disengagement from some people and activities that drain our energy also allows us to redirect that energy to more worthy purposes. Stress and adversity is part of our lives (and not a bad thing), but we have to question if the stress and adversity are increasing our energy or draining it. Investment management (time and energy) drives our ability to maximize learning, growth, and productivity. We control only ourselves.

Moving Forward

> If you can't fly then run, if you can't run then walk, if you can't walk then crawl, but whatever you do, you have to keep moving forward.
>
> Martin Luther King, Jr.

We start from where we begin. Erase yesterday and tomorrow. Live. Our path forward is influenced and controlled by many things in our daily life. We don't have control of a large part of how our world works. In contrast, we have substantial control over how we interact with the world around us and how the world impacts our emotions, thoughts, feelings, and behaviors.

We previously assessed our own characteristics to better understand our "today's starting point." Each of us will excel in some areas and score poorly in other areas. The characteristics are generally categorized for understanding to help us address areas that we might improve. Let's delve more deeply into our personal models of wisdom.

> *Who are the wise people in your world?*
> *Why do you personally consider them wise?*

The wise people in our lives will color our perception of what wise means. Take a few minutes to carefully consider each person in turn. Assess the person(s) in the three major categories of understanding of self, understanding of others, and knowledge and experience. While you certainly can't assess a person's thoughts, feelings, or emotions, you can assess your perception of personal mastery and interaction with others. We have few models in our lives, so we need to better understand the qualities that we want to emulate in ourselves.

> How does their knowledge impact their interactions? What are their limitations? How do they apply their knowledge to different situations? How do they communicate and interact? How do they inspire and share?
>
> How does their formative experience impact their view of the world? Which experience is critical in their story? How do they relate their experience? How does their experience help them chart a course of action? How do they leverage their experience to solve unknown problems?
>
> Why are you drawn to the person's wisdom? What characteristics allow them to influence you and others? Does benevolence,

empathy, honesty, humbleness impact their communication with others? Do they self-sacrifice to serve others? What do they gain by helping others?

Do they have self-mastery? What is their belief structure? What drives them to grow and be productive? How do they persevere in adverse situations? How do they balance personal mindfulness while remaining productive? How do they continue to grow?

This list of questions provides a start point to begin reverse engineering your personal idea of wisdom. We need to know where we are (our start) and where we are going (our finish).

Remarkable people are well documented and relatively easy to study. The following are a few exemplar individuals who have been widely recognized for their wisdom. Here's some of those:

Maya Angelou Winston Churchill, Marie Curie, Daryl Davis, Ann Frank, Mahatma Gandhi, Jane Goodall, Martin Luther King, Jr., Abraham Lincoln, Nelson Mandela, Theodore Roosevelt, Mother Teresa, Wangarĩ Maathai, Malala Yousafzai

It's not a list of perfect people, nor is it a comprehensive list. Others may come to mind who may have impacted you because of their remarkable character. Each has admirable qualities and impacts not only individuals but also communities and society.

What traits are shared between these remarkable individuals?
What traits are unique?

Mentors foster wisdom; they don't give wisdom or teach wisdom. We each have models of wisdom in our life and remarkably wise people that we can use as an aspirational goal.

It would be wonderful if an individualized roadmap to wisdom was available, but we know that it's not that simple. Why? First, there simply isn't a valid and reliable measure to determine who is wise. Will there ever be one? Second, the saying of "They broke the mold after creating that one" is likely the easiest to understand when we talk of the wise. When you review the list of remarkably wise people, you find very different backgrounds, experience, knowledge, and personalities – and each person has their flaws. Finally, the wise in our life live and demonstrate traits that we admire and hope to learn.

Why are they wise? Because we consider them wise. We consider them wise within the context of our lives. We observe and are a part of the wise decisions that they make in their everyday lives, the compassion that they show to others, the challenges that they overcome, and their generosity in sharing what they have learned. You will find characteristics of the remarkably wise are mirrored in the wise people of our life. Understanding these admirable qualities is a first step in moving forward in the study of wisdom.

Of the 7.9 billion people on the earth there is no one in the world with your backstory. You are unique. No one grew up in your shoes. No one else lived in your mind. No one was involved in your self-talk. No one viewed your experience through your lens of the world. Our parents, closest family, friends, and loved ones don't know our intimately held personal opinions, feelings, and thoughts that we don't share for fear of being misunderstood.

It's surprising to hear from those closest to you that "you've changed." It's surprising because we never notice it personally. It's akin to a pressure that builds below the surface and builds to a critical mass. The world only experiences a sudden earthquake that changes the surrounding landscape. These changes create new attitudes and destroy old models. It's not that we weren't aware that we were changing our course, changing our attitude, or changing our relations. Change happens over time and, sometimes, over a very long time. Our daily wise decision-making creates change that results in breakthroughs.

The following is a visioning exercise to better understand your personal goal. Complete these visioning exercises through the lens of building personal wisdom:

> *Short term*
> *Who do you want to be in ten years?*
> *What differences will others perceive in a decade?*
> *How will you change your impact on individuals and the community?*
> *Long term*
> *Who do you want to be at the end of your life?*
> *What do you want everyone to remember about you in 100 years?*
> *What will others say about your impact on individuals and the community?*

These are deep introspective questions designed to consider the destination. It's difficult to understand the circumstances of our past. Our past can haunt the present and impede future growth.

With an average life span of 79 years in the United States, we have a limited time on the earth to make an impact. We must grow and change. Ten years is a long time to make a change – imagine focusing on understanding yourself for four years (the span of a college degree). What might you learn and accomplish in four years? What about taking four years to delve into understanding others? How might you grow? What might change? What do you need to grow? Without growth, stagnation is the only outcome.

Creating your plan

In a wisdom growth model, we are striving to create a wide and deep diversity of experiences and lessons learned that fosters an exponential growth in personal wisdom and outruns the natural process of growing older. It requires an understanding of the behavior, characteristics, and traits of the wise and a systematic focus on growing in our areas of weakness. Each wise person has a mixture of unique characteristics and has a different ability to leverage each. To grow, we must keep a humble understanding of what we know and more importantly what we do not know as we become exponentially better at self-reflection and grow in personal agency. Wise is rare and worthy of our time (Figure 4.2).

The big question: Can I become wise? Yes. Maybe. It depends. The wise didn't reach a point where they could put "wise" on their resume, nor did they gain a certificate of achievement. A culmination of many personal traits, behavioral characteristics, life experience, and knowledge provided them the opportunity to progress their understanding of themselves and others.

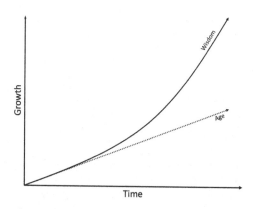

Figure 4.2 Age and wisdom divergence.

Growing Wisdom

We have to first have absolute honesty with ourselves. We stay in our comfort zones because this is exactly how it sounds: comfortable. We are content, relaxed, and have the amenities that we enjoy. There's nothing wrong with being in the comfort zone, if that's exactly where you want to be. Our difficulty is that this comfort zone soothes and puts us into a mode of complacency that can lead to stagnation. Most of the time, we are relaxing when we are not yet at our destination – we are not yet where we want to be. Sometimes we're simply tired, stressed, and need to reenergize and reevaluate. It's the comfortable chair in the living room that tempts you to sit down – and seemingly holds you until you are forced to take that mid-afternoon nap. There is nothing inherently wrong with comfort, but we are trying to build a depth and breadth of experience that fosters personal wisdom.

We need to move from comfort and complacency to learning and growth. This involves confronting our fears and finding motivation to learn and grow.

To move out of our comfort zone, we must confront two things: motivation and fear. Our motivation can be extrinsic (e.g., goal, competition, bonuses, promotion, praise), intrinsic (curiosity, satisfaction, learning, mastery, pride), or a combination of both. Our fear of challenge may come in the form of lack of confidence, opinions of others, possibility of failure, humiliation, and lack of skill. Whether starting a new sport, a podcast, a promotion, learning a language, moving to a new culture, planting a garden, or starting new relationships. Our motivation and fear are palatable, and we confront the barrier to moving out of our personal comfort zone. Feel fear and move forward bravely.

A jack of all trades is a master of none, but oftentimes better than a master of one.

This adage is often shortened and misinterpreted. Having a depth and breadth of interest and skill, while not being an expert in anything, can be advantageous as it applies to wisdom. While a master has a depth of knowledge surpassing others in their field, the breadth (application) of that knowledge can be quite narrow due to time and effort in the specialization. A jack of all trades, in our vernacular today, would be referred to as a generalist. The generalist is sufficient in knowledge and flexible in application and ability.

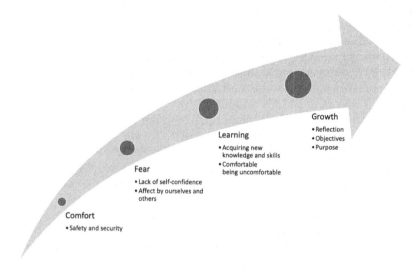

Figure 4.3 Growth spectrum.

In our global knowledge economy, we might consider the following: "Jack of all trades and a master of one." Developing a mastery in one area and having broad knowledge in many related areas. We need to get comfortable being uncomfortable acquiring new knowledge, skills, attitudes, and ability. Our ability to adapt and change can be seen in the rapid growth of job markets and opportunities that didn't exist 10 or 20 years ago (e.g., social media managers, bloggers, virtual assistants, data scientists) (Figure 4.3).

SELF-IMPOSED CHALLENGE

Adversity, challenge, and diverse experience are the basic ingredients for growth. There are many challenges and adversities that enter our lives that we can only endure and overcome. For many, adversity is considered a barrier to success rather than a leverage for wisdom. Challenge is an *advantage* as it relates to wisdom.

Self-imposed challenges are proactive activities to push ourselves outside of our comfort zone and grow. It's designed to see how we apply previous learning in a different way. It is our attempt to move ourselves out of our current way of thinking or living to make discoveries about ourselves. The application of challenge can come in many different forms: Mental, physical, emotional, or spiritual.

We cannot always change our job or change our life. We can seek challenge that grows our knowledge of ourselves and others and increases the depth and breadth of our knowledge and experience:

Travel helps us with our relationships with others. It opens our mind to different cultures, societies, people, philosophies, and languages. It forces us to be mindful of ourselves and our reaction to the world around us. We become aware of different ways of approaching life that are fundamentally different from our own yet provide contentment and enrichment.

Meditation and Solitude help us understand ourselves better. Our meaning and purpose quickly find an expansive place that allows contemplation, evaluation, and development. Meditation and solitude provide us with the opportunity for uninterrupted self-talk to understand ourselves and find peace in our own presence. Emotional and spiritual energy impacts our feelings, thoughts, and behavior which affect our happiness and contentment. Successful management is closely aligned with self-efficacy and provides us self-governance, confidence, purposefulness, and growth.

Physical Activity helps to decrease cognitive decline (psychological age) and can positively affect blood glucose levels, aerobic capacity (VO_2), blood pressure, muscle strength, and immune functions. Physical activity and the associated energy renewal through physical fitness, nutrition, and recovery provide the ability to increase our productivity and emotional self-governance.

Leverage self-challenge to build wisdom. Build your own adversity.

Whether you spend miles of running, hours strumming a guitar, smashing a tennis ball, moving iron weights, or building a yoga sweat it is time well spent. The regulation of our thought, feeling, and emotion will lead to pair behavior. Amateur marathon runners don't often have strong external motivations. Thoughts of medals, peer pressure, and accolades fade quickly as the training becomes overwhelming. The miles of training find the athlete with the aches and pains of physical effort, crowded with self-talk and feeling. Mastering the physical pains, emotional self-talk, and balancing life are juggled during the highs and lows of the marathon training to build our self-agency.

Adversity and challenge strain our ability to control the emotions of our failure and the brilliance of our small successes. Adversity is to humans as fertilizer is to plants. Adversity can be leveraged to grow our understanding of ourselves and our understanding of others. Without adversity and self-challenge there's little to motivate us to move beyond our comfort zone to courageously grow and learn.

Introspection

Introspection is self-examination, focused to look at our own emotions, feelings, and behavior to consider our personal motivation. Even the best laid plans get changed. External influences impact our emotions, feelings, thoughts, and behavior, but they don't control us.

We each have a different story that has brought us here, to today. It's a story that has already been told, and it leaves an impression on our life. This backstory doesn't control our future.

We travel our life by ourselves and pick up traveling partners along the way. Our travel partners may be family, friends, colleagues, teammates, or random strangers that travel our same path for a time. We mourn for the loss of some, remember the fond ones, and pick up new companions. We gather a loose band of individuals that help us grow. Stay on your journey – don't worry for those who aren't on the same path. The path to wisdom has been walked by others before us, but it's certainly a road less traveled. Keep working on you. We will gain knowledge and experience as we move forward and build relationships that grow in our understanding of others. We will encounter adversity that forces us to learn, evolve, and grow. We also find wise mentors that become our valued partners in our journey.

The innate ability to learn, grow, and become wise is invaluable. It's not good enough to be good enough. Our global knowledge economy will change the way we value people and organizations. Our job may not exist in 20 years.

The industrial revolution changed agrarian cultures by using machines for repetitive tasks, rather than people. The cotton gin, spinning jenny, and the development of factories had sweeping social and economic implications. Today, we are in the middle of a digital revolution led by rapid development of machine learning and artificial intelligence. This innovation will lead to further gains in efficiency and productivity. At the same time, we are left to wonder about the implications on our personal lives, communities, and society when information and knowledge is harnessed by technology.

Wisdom is uniquely human. It is universally valued and will remain a uniquely human resource of the future.

Part Two

Collective Wisdom

5 A Mentoring Relationship

Mentoring Wise Behavior

Part One provided a perspective on fostering individual wisdom and created a foundation for understanding the difference between training for knowledge and fostering the growth of wisdom for individuals. As discussed earlier, we are each uniquely the same. This principle provides mentors a solid foundation to create common purpose and shared values and to foster growth in wisdom at the individual, system, and organizational levels.

The focus of Part Two is to help foster collective wisdom in organizations. Our organizations are filled with knowledgeable workers and our human resource development scholars have long-proven models to help us train individuals effectively. The central idea of building wisdom in organizations is to build a workforce that can think and grow. Collective wisdom is not simply shared knowledge, though it's a great start, but it's building a workforce that learns and grows together.

> *Collective wisdom is a shared understanding of wise behaviors that are collected and curated by an interconnected group to create a beneficial course of action for the group, communities, and society.*

The access to information and knowledge is extraordinary. The critical skills needed by employees today are not technical skills, but soft skills: accountability, adaptability, critical thinking, creativity, communication, desire to learn, drive, ethics, flexibility, positive attitude, social skills, systematic thinking, teamwork, and literacy. This list isn't meant to be exhaustive, and many of these skills have been desired since the beginning of employment. Yet, these are the skills that we most often struggle to improve in our organizations. This list of soft skills is not job dependent. These skills, minimally, are required

DOI: 10.4324/9781003018759-7

for productive cooperative work in our global knowledge economy. Training can remedy technical skills, but the soft skills are difficult to develop without an investment in time and energy.

Our understanding of employee motivation has changed with giant leaps of understanding in leadership, organizational development, and social psychology. In the 1950s and 1960s Douglas McGregor described Theory X and Theory Y leadership theories with Abraham Maslow contributing Theory Z in the late 1960s. These theories directed that those employees could be divided into three major categories: employees who avoid work, employees looking for opportunities to work, and employees who work for improvement. In a parallel effort, Edward Deming, Joseph Juran, and Philip Crosby approached employee development from a continuous improvement direction focusing on work effort and quality of results.

Robert Greenleaf, in "The Servant as Leader," (1970), argued that leaders should "serve" their followers. This was a dramatic departure and an upside downing of traditional leadership. Greenleaf wrote, "The Servant-Leader is servant first. It begins with the natural feeling that one wants to serve, to serve first. Then conscious choice brings one to aspire to lead. The difference manifests itself in the care taken by the servant-first to make sure that other people's highest priority needs are being served. Do those serve grow as persons? Do they, while being served, become healthier, wiser, freer, more autonomous, more likely themselves to become servants? And what is the effect on the least privileged in society; will they benefit, or, at least, not be further deprived?" (p. 6). Servant leadership was a dramatic and defining departure from classic leadership theories to not look at the profitability but to look to the care of the heart of the organization – its people.

Twenty years later (1990), thought leaders such as Peter Senge (a systems scientist) introduced the idea of the "learning organization" and created an understanding of the interconnectedness of units and processes in the organization. This was our first examination of the systems of organizations. We began not only looking at organizational charts but also interrelated relationships that move across the organization and between units and individuals. This was a dramatic departure from the idea of people as a tool or machine of the organization used for productivity, popularizing the idea of personal mastery as part of the larger competitive advantage of the organization. The early 1990s was a time of change for organizations, and it created a "call to action" for companies to transform themselves into learning organizations. This change was not for the employees, or leaders, but as a systematic process of growing the organization through the growth of all employees and systems. In much the same way, 30 years later, our organizations have a better understanding of how to curate collective learning, but there remains little understanding of how to foster individual wisdom while building and curating collective wisdom. We explore how mentors can serve to foster wisdom in the workplace.

Guidepost

We are personally responsible for building our knowledge, skills, and attitudes to maximize our competence. We shape our growth through self-efficacy and personal agency to learn from previous experience and plan next steps. Our opportunities for learning moments and growth are endless.

Competency is acquired and inspired with curiosity, reading, research, practice, observation, participation, interaction, reflection, abstract thinking, learning, unlearning, and perspective. We are accountable for our learning and growth, and it's dependent on our drive, motivation, and perseverance. We are active contextual learners who learn best through personal interaction and experience rather than by reading. Through growth and adaptation, we learn self-reliance, resilience, and how to best communicate to build relationships. We connect new knowledge with our own understandings of ourselves and others and through the contextual lens of our own experiences.

We leverage our learning through our relations with others. Humans are primates that live and learn together by interacting with others and working cooperatively to investigate and solve problems. We learn best when we learn cooperatively with others.

There are special people in our lives that serve as guideposts and guiding lights as our teachers, mentors, and mentoring partners. We leverage their knowledge and experiences to enhance our own self-growth. We mutually share knowledge and experiences to enhance the relationship. We have the pleasure to share time with many special people who become friends, colleagues, and mentoring partners. We recognize a very special few as our wise mentors. These partnerships can last from moment to years and help reflect.

Mentors are trusted and competent guides who model, listen, foster, influence, and inspire others to achieve a goal or purpose. Our mentors, guides, gurus, and leaders assist us in growing our knowledge and wisdom through strategic thinking and complex analysis of a changing world. Are mentors required? No. Mentors are not a requirement for growth in wisdom but can foster the learning process. As children, we interact, participate, and observe our family and friends to create models and theories of our world – our first experience with mentors. As we advance through middle childhood and teenage years, the interactions, observations, and activity participation stretch to include larger segments of our community and society. For most of our adolescent and adult lives, we live in a wicked learning environment that provides false positives, little feedback, and enforcement of harsh feedback when we make a mistake. We live in a world that is not bound by rules, instant and reliable feedback, and positive reinforcement. Sometimes feedback and reinforcement are not kind and not helpful – in a wicked way. Our mentors have experience in these wicked environments, and we chose our mentors based on our evaluation of their contextual wisdom or specialized expertise.

Our mentors, guides, and gurus provide us the opportunity to learn through their own understanding, knowledge, and experience. We consider them wise within the context of our lives. We observe, and are a part of, the wise decisions that they make in their everyday life, the compassion that they show to others, the challenges that they overcome, and their generosity in sharing what they have learned.

Mentors are found or discovered rather than provided. A mentor's sound judgment is harvested from life experience, learning, observations, failure, and overcoming adversity. Their added "value" comes not only from their knowledge, but their ability to listen, understand, interpret, and provide insight, inspiration, and individual compassion. Understanding and growing in knowledge and understanding requires guides who have lived in wicked learning environments, learned the lessons, and can provide relatable guidance to individuals learning to strive and thrive in these chaotic environments.

In explaining mentoring, mountain climbing has the most similarities. We each learn to climb a mountain a little bit at a time, a little different path, a little different rate of speed, and at a little different interest level. Our mountain climbing starts with the biggest local "mountain" in our region. Our local mountains are both challenging for our level ability but achievable. They are normally well labeled and have one to three footpaths to the top. They offer a relatively kind learning environment. Sneakers and sandals – no problem. Complete with a concrete path, handrails when needed, and a convenient bench and water fountain. No map – no problem. We have trail signs along the trail. No flashlight – no problem. Lights are positioned along the trail. This isn't to minimize the accomplishment of a local climbing or hike, it simply is a kind learning experience where mistakes are minimized by the safety nets (water, light). We are provided strong immediate feedback for questions through direction and paths. For most people, this kind learning environment lets them self-learn and become more self-reliant as a hiker and climber. Those who climb the really big mountains can normally no longer count the number of small mountains that they have climbed in their history, but the experience and lessons learned on those climbs are invaluable as they encounter more challenges.

At some point in a climber's career, it becomes more challenging. It might be 4401.2m Mount Ebert in America, 5894m Kilimanjaro in Africa, 8848.86m Everest at the China–Nepal border, or the ultimate savage mountain K2 at 8611m on the China–Pakistan border. We cannot always rely on self-learning. The risk of injury or death during a climb will require climbers to seek guidance and support. In many cases, we must unlearn our climbing models of the past and adopt new models that are more appropriate to our new climbing environment.

We, of course, learn a lot on our own via trial and error, observation, and education. But often we can leverage the knowledge and experience of guides and mentors that have "been there and done that." In mountain climbing, the value of mentorship grows as the cost of mistakes inflates. A lack of understanding higher altitude preparation (medical, clothing, food, water, weather, rockslides, and cliff hugging selfies) leads to the death of a surprising number of individuals each year. We must be self-learning while also seeking, investigating solutions, and resourcing experts. In addition, we must take advantage of the mountain experts who have lived their lives in a wicked learning environment where mistakes can mean death.

Mentoring (guides, Sherpas, and expedition teams) creates a safety net for the novice in a wicked mountain environment. Our mentors in climbing can be fellow travelers, veteran climbers who know the mountain, professional climbers, or professional expedition leaders. Not everyone seeks or needs a guide for many of their experiences, but there comes a point that the risk of failure overrides our ability to survive the encounter and try the mountain another day.

Mountains are a wonderful analogy for a life journey or for fostering wisdom. We are accountable for our journey. Nature is a wild card in the same way that trauma, adversity, and challenges can sideline our plans for success. We optimistically handle the delays, detours, and disasters to find another course to our destination. We override the emotions to master the feelings, thoughts, and behaviors to move courageously forward. We seek loved ones, counselors, mentors, and teachers to move forward to the top of the mountain.

Mentoring

You choose your path then choose your mentors, wisely. Each of us, throughout our lives, looks to mentors to assist us in our life's journey. In our early childhood, this most often takes the form of our parents and relatives (mentors) who help raise us. We (mentees) learn, from our mentors, the basics of life during our formative childhood. While these mentors are often chosen from among those in our immediate life, during early adolescence we begin choosing our mentors from a wider circle of our community that may also include teachers, clergy, friends, and coworkers. This doesn't necessarily remove early mentors but serves to widen our circle of mentors.

The roles of mentor and mentee are convenient titles. The mentoring is often observed as a one-way relationship where the mentor is providing sage advice and the mentee is receiving sage advice. The mentor/mentee view of the mentorship works for some, but it's usually best left to adult–child situations where mentoring more closely resembles informal teaching.

In the following, we explore mentoring from four different perspectives.

Resource as Mentoring

Though we might consider reading to be a solitary activity, books are a fantastic way to access knowledge across distance, time, race, and culture to learn from others what we might never discover in our own short life. We find experts, and the writing of the wise accessible, as they curated knowledge waiting to be shared. Aristotle, in *Nicomachean Ethics*, Book 6 writes, "Wisdom must plainly be the most finished of the forms of knowledge." Our short life doesn't allow us the ability to study at the feet of this philosopher in 340 B.C.E. (2.4 millennium ago), but the documentation of his work allows us to read, study, and reinterpret this knowledge for our modern society. The cumulative knowledge and collective wisdom of countless generations is accessible at our fingertips.

It sounds strange to name "books" as a mentoring pathway, but the writings and legacy of Plato, Aristotle, Socrates, Marcus Aurelius, Musashi Miyamoto, Jane Austen, Leo Tolstoy, Thomas Paine, George Orwell, Tony Morrison, and many others have assisted generations of readers with changing themselves and their world. Covey's "The 7 Habits of Highly Effective People," Carnegie's "How to Win Friends and Influence People," Peter's "Thriving on Chaos," and Garner's "Multiple Intelligences" have provided sage mentorship, reaching the heights of popularity by prescribing how we might think about ourselves and our interaction with a changing world.

The writings of these skilled authors and mentors have reached across borders and across generations providing belief structures, courage, empathy, inspiration, and influence for others to grow and change themselves, their community, and society. Far too many wise humans who have remained undocumented as such over the generations. Their wisdom is left to only those who they touch in their life. Their wisdom often becomes oral history that is told as lessons to the next generation of social learners.

To paraphrase Hans Christian Andersen, the wiser a person becomes, the more they will read, and those who are wisest read most. Imagination provides an opportunity for abstract thinking and reflection. Our stories, fables, and fairy tales provide tales of adversity, success, inspiration that describe human ambition, failures, ideals, dreams and have built our archetypes of wisdom (Yoda, Fairy Godmother, Gilda, Gandalf).

We use documented resources for extending our observational experience. It allows us to travel in our imagination to other locations, to experience other cultures, to delve into new ways of thinking, and to extrapolate how to use this knowledge to better ourselves. We see in our authors a documentation of success and failure and their advice for navigating in an uncertain world. This is passive but valuable mentoring and depends on us to both learn and unlearn.

Leaders as Mentors

Wise leaders foster individual wisdom while building and curating collective wisdom. This requires leaders that inspire and influence others. Kind and ethical leaders support, influence, and inspire their community. Our formal and informal leaders utilize their communication skills to listen and to foster growth in both individuals and the larger community. Leaders need a strong sense of accountability coupled with knowledge and experience needed to make sound judgments and to chart a strategic and flexible course of action for the community.

Formal Leaders

When individuals describe the wise in their lives, seldom do they describe a boss, supervisor, administrator, or other hierarchical leader. This isn't a criticism of leadership but represents a clear distinction between wise mentors and leaders. Can leaders mentor? Yes, absolutely.

They should, and must, mentor new generations of leaders within the organization for succession planning. They should be mentoring for career growth and development for themselves and others. They should be mentoring to nurture job satisfaction and retention to attract and retain high-quality employees.

Hierarchical leadership in organizations is an assigned job title, and the leader is burdened with responsibilities of deadlines, bottom lines, and accountability for the achievement and failures of those within their area of responsibility. Often leaders do not connect mentoring to organizational outcome because it is difficult to measure and analyze the impact the mentoring has at a business level. Higher rates of job satisfaction and employee retention can be obtained through mentoring. Company culture is strengthened through mentorship. Skills are increased at a faster rate with mentorship. We increase credibility between leaders and followers through mentorship. Capacity of empathy, communication, patience, sharing, trust, and objectivity are increased with mentorship.

Leaders with empathy and listening skills can develop relationships that provide rich opportunities to inspire and influence. As social creatures, humans respect their leadership for their knowledge, skills, and benevolence. We cannot lead without influencing people, and we cannot mentor without understanding people.

Organizational culture is a dynamic set of patterns, values, behaviors, and perceptions that are learned and shared by a group of people. Leaders, both formal and informal, have a tremendous influence on the culture, organization, systems, and people. Organizational culture is described as a gift when it's positive and a curse when it's negative. Organizational culture is not dichotomous, nor is it an object that we can touch, measure, and manipulate on a day-to-day basis.

Primal leadership advocates that a leader's emotional intelligence has a tremendous influence on organization culture, thus impacting the business results. Social leadership advocates collaboration, open and collaborative community, social networking, and shared ideas. This growing perspective of leadership theory allows leaders, both formal and informal, to mentor, build social skills, influence, inspire, and lead. These two perspectives of leadership provide a fantastic base for leadership development and a key to moving organizational culture forward.

Informal Leaders

Informal leaders are often overlooked but can serve, if supported, as natural resources for mentorship activities. Informal leaders often have natural social communication skills, possess a strong understanding of others, and are competent, creditable, sharing, influential, and collaborative. Informal leaders build relationships that ignore the organizational hierarchy to connect with a diverse cadre of individuals. These leaders understand the formal and informal systems and structure within the organization and can find a course of action to find solutions. Often, these leaders are abstract and creative thinkers who can positively impact new initiatives.

Informal leaders have advantages that are different from formal leaders. They have natural skills that are not attached to a job title. They understand how the organization functions. They are considered credible, share easily, and are competent, influential, and often inspirational. In addition, they often think outside the box and readily adapt to positive change. These informal leaders are well positioned and naturally skilled to become mentoring partners.

It's a critical goal to build a workforce of wise leaders that are competent, influential, inspirational, compassionate, open-minded, innovative, and efficient. Our formal and informal leaders must be our frontline mentoring partners.

Teachers as Mentors

Teachers and trainers are often talked about in synonymous terms. Teachers help learners acquire and improve a broad knowledge, skill, and attitudes while trainers help learners acquire and improve specific and applied knowledge and skills. Further, education is a systematic process of learning with the goal of acquiring knowledge, skills, or changing attitude, while training is a process of learning with the goal of acquiring a skill or behavior. Teaching and training are complementary and share the goal of building competency; however, the teachers and trainers are not necessarily mentors. As teachers and trainers, we need to narrate why the subject is important to us, teach the content and context of the subject matter, guide practice, and foster exploration and discovery. Our methods and techniques of teaching and training are important and help us connect and develop trusting relationships. Effective teaching and training involve several important roles that become an important foundation to building relationships. The role of teacher or trainer is not the most important role.

Teachers and trainers help learners acquire competence by improving knowledge, skill, and attitudes. Building a learner's competence leads to confidence and competence and confidence equates to capability.

A teacher or trainer is most often required to be the sage on the stage, teaching the content and context of the subject matter. It's not that they don't want to mentor, but the time restriction and over-whelming materials require that they cover "just the facts." When this is asked, they are hampered and unable to create a foundation of men-torship through narration, coaching, and advising their learners.

Narratives provide understanding and reasoning for the student. As learners, we often are in a classroom with very little reason for learning the information being delivered. As contextual learners and social learners, we need a reason for learning. Learners need to un-derstand why the information is important to them. The teacher is the prescribed expert on the subject and has their own reason for teaching the content. We, as learners, need to understand why we need to learn what is being taught to us. It's important that the teacher or trainer provide a narrative reason why the information is important to the learner. This is the trainer's first step in developing a trusting relation-ship with the learner. By crafting and narrating previous experiences, context for the lesson, and application of the material (long or short term) to the student, the teacher opens a connection between them-selves, the material, and the learner. This external motivation by the teacher/trainer influences and inspires the student to listen and open themselves to the content that will grow their competence and capabil-ities. When we teach, we share our experiences, stories, truths, paths, and techniques. Does that mean we're right? Of course not, it's just easier to learn from other's bad judgments before trying it yourself for the first time. There will be fewer bruises from the attempt.

Practice, Practice, Practice. A classroom, or mentored environment is a nursery for building a learner's sound judgment. While we do learn by listening, we learn best by experiencing. Guided practice provides the learner to experience what has been taught. Case studies, simula-tions, labs, and internships are just a few examples of practice experi-ences. Sound judgment is forged through a long series of good and bad judgments. Learners should be afforded the opportunity to be right and to be wrong. If a learner is always right, there is little adversity/challenge and therefore little opportunity to grow their personal wis-dom. If a learner is wrong, the challenge may be overwhelming, and they have an opportunity to seek assistance, build relationships, and better understand their capability. We seek assistance to discover how to correct future decisions. We learn from our good judgment (our suc-cesses), we learn from our bad judgment (failures), and we learn how others make decisions. We want our pilots, engineers, teachers, and ironworkers (everyone) to build their competence, intuition, insight, self-reliance, experience, and resilience. These shared learning experi-ences in success and failure build trust and develop empathy. Practice provides the teacher/trainer the opportunity to mentor through a coaching role as the student practices the correct steps and processes.

Fostered exploration and discovery are an integral part of the learning experiences. Exploration and discovery are driven by the questions of "What if?" It is a key to building a mentoring relationship. The teacher can serve in an advising role to the student building abstract reasons and systematic thinking skills. As social learners, we grow by interacting with others and working cooperatively to investigate and solve problems. Our advisors offer corrective action, share experiences, and provide counsel. We have a developed fear of failure and being wrong. Being wrong and failing is part of growing. We cannot teach people to not fear, but we can teach people to be brave. Exploration and discovery are filled with overwhelming failure and wild success that develops trust, confidence, and self-reliance.

Exploration and discovery in a learning environment provides opportunities to fail and a path to success. Exploration and discovery are best when we leverage learning with other's experiences. Sometimes, as learners, we just simply need an ear and a discussion. Not a problem resolved, or an issue solved. We need some interaction, discussion, and help to create a course of action leading to beneficial and productive decisions.

It's a critical goal to build a workforce of competent and capable employees that are self-reliant and efficient and have the capacity to work with others to create an innovative and efficient workspace. Our teachers, trainers, and HR professionals are our natural organizational mentors, but it is a role that every mentoring partner uses to foster wisdom in themselves and others.

Mentor/mentee Relationship

As social learners, collaborative mentoring is a very natural way that we learn and socialize. Everyday mentoring happens between friends, parents, teachers, colleagues, leaders, and team members. These mentoring relationships help to build better relationships and leverage learning, share experiences, and build capacity. Formal mentoring happens when we screen a mentoring partner, then select and train individuals for collective success.

Mentoring is an often undervalued activity which has some inherent assumptions that we need to overcome to develop true collaborative mentoring relationships. Informal mentorship happens every day and within every organization. These informal mentoring relationships often naturally occur from developing relationships between peers.

Within the workplace these informal mentorships often fill the information and knowledge gap that is missed during formal education and training opportunities.

Jimi Hendrix famously stated, "Knowledge speaks, wisdom listens." Our traditional mentoring frameworks prescribe the role of mentor and mentee. Mentors share their knowledge and experience with mentees, and they wisely listen. Mentors inspire the mentee through their activities and influence through their action to build confidence, competence, and capacity. In addition, mentors often have a depth and breadth of understanding of relationships and have a well-developed understanding of self. These are virtues that they can foster in their mentees. Thus, foster future generations of wise mentors.

These wise mentors are sought for their mentorship due to domain experience, communication skills and influence. Mentor listens with empathy, confidentiality, and compassion. They are aware of the mentee's needs. The best of our mentors asks the two questions "How can I best serve this mentee?" and "How can I make this mentee a better version of themselves?

Mentees are seekers. For the most part, in adult mentoring, the mentee comes into a relationship searching for answers. Much in the same was in the martial arts that a student might seek a master. Mentees are often the best of students. They are entering the relationship open to change, open to criticism, open to advice, and open to revelation. Mentees are seekers of knowledge so that they can better navigate their chosen path. Mentees guide discovery through questioning. Mentees gather information with their communication skills. Finally, the mentee interprets the mentor's advice and council so that it can be applied for their personal circumstances.

While this is a standard relationship in a mentor, it can become stagnant and burdensome for both the mentor and mentee. The roles are set. The mentor provides (teacher role) and the mentee receives (student role). While there are differences between mentor and teachers, this type of relationship is parallel to an education or coaching relationship rather than fully utilizing the cooperative mentoring relationship.

Collaborative Mentoring

Mentoring is a guarded two-way relationship, based on mutual trust, between two or more mentoring partners where both members share and nurture growth of knowledge, experiences, and an understanding. Mentorship should be a protected relationship that supports and develops all members. Collaborative mentoring requires shared purpose, opportunities for growth, open communication, and confidentiality.

Mentoring partnerships should acknowledge that each person in the relationship has an equal role in the relationship and that all individuals have goals that can be achieved through a collaborative partnership.

Mentoring partnerships should not be singular endeavors, but an engaged activity of the workplace culture. Humans can adapt, learn, and evolve individually, but as social creatures we also readily learn from not only our own experiences but by learning from the experiences of others. We find belonging, support, understanding, and engagement in our social communities which allow us to learn and grow faster from the mentorship of others.

We have four major types of social relationships that can be used to better understand mentoring and mentoring relationships: one-to-one, one-to-many, many-to-one, and many-to-many relationships. Each member of our workplace brings a unique perspective to the workforce through their competencies, capabilities, and capacity to understand and interact with others. As engaged members of a community, each member can support, protect, and further the growth of their community. This forms the basis for rich mentoring programs.

Our communities are living organisms that seldom stay in a steady state of health, rather they are either improving or declining. We each have an active role to play in maintaining and growing the health of the community through our roles as formal and informal leaders and engaged colleagues. Shared purpose of cohesion, culture, performance, and growth each play a special role in influencing the health and well-being of this living organism.

It's difficult to defend the assignment of mentors. The assignment of a mentor to a mentee is indicative that a mentor is in charge and the mentee follows. In this type of relationship, the mentee is the receiver of knowledge, and the mentor is the provider of knowledge. In this situation, it's easy to see "what's in it for me" from the mentee perspective – knowledge. However, it's difficult to find an internal motivation, other than altruism, for the assigned mentor. For the most part, an assigned mentor is akin to individualize instruction by a teacher or trainer. In this scenario, the mentor is inherently in charge and is tasked with educating or training the mentee. We should choose our mentoring partners. Collaborative mentoring is a guarded two-way relationship, based on mutual trust, respect, and optimism. Ethics, belief systems, empathy, compassion, generosity, and trust are prerequisites to building a relationship and seldom is assigned mentorship an appropriate first step.

Growing

Collective wisdom is a shared understanding of wise behaviors that are collected and curated by an interconnected group to create a beneficial course of action for the group, communities, and society.

Our diverse workplace communities are rich in knowledge and wisdom. Too often we look through the silos of an organization, rather than across systems of the organization. Our community (collective) mentoring should be involved in both individual and collective career development. Our community mentoring should be involved in both individual and collective personal development. Our community mentoring should create a sense of belonging and shared purpose toward engagement. Finally, our community mentoring should develop leaders that inspire and use influence toward the communities shared purpose.

We foster wisdom by first fostering wise decisions and behaviors to forward a shared purpose. The knowledge, experience, and wisdom in our workforce is rich and seldom utilized with a purpose to grow our workplace and workforce. We need wise mentors. "Wise" is free of job title or rank. There are no age requirements. There is no educational requirement. There are no race or cultural requirements. There are no religious or nonreligious requirements. There is no location/geographic requirement for wisdom.

Wisdom is contextual within a community. There is no ownership of the subjects, only lenses that are used to explore and grow in wisdom.

6 Workplace Resilience, Adaptability, and Connection

We are globally workforce connected across time zones, economies, and culture. It's very difficult for most of us to define where our work life begins and where our personal life ends. From a very personal perspective, our emotions, feelings, thoughts, and behavior travel with us without regard to whether we are at work or in our personal space. Today, due to our knowledge economy, we have skewed and blurred much of the line between the workplace and our personal spaces. Our relationships extend from the office to 24 hours online social communities that ignore the hierarchy of the organizations and society. Is this good or bad? We don't know yet. It just is. We are not going to go backwards. We move forward with the technology and the changes that it forces on traditional societal norms of communication. The creation of the World Wide Web 30 years ago dramatically changed the way we think about the world. A global pandemic in 2020 changed organizational landscapes and left employees and organizations scrambling to find new ways to work, new ways to live, new ways to better the quality of our lives, and new measures of success and satisfaction.

Every individual is looking for avenues to improve themselves. Every organization seeks improvement as well. The individual's and organization's measures of improvement may look very different. The measure of success of individuals is not typically a good third quarter, while the measure of success for an organization is not typically more time on a hammock in the woods. Abraham Maslow would argue that individuals have five major needs: physiological, safety, love and belonging, esteem, and self-actualization. Organizations have needs too: efficiency, cash flow, customer satisfaction, impact (mission), and reputation (values).

The truism of human experience paralleling that of organizations is evident during hard times, we find that people and organizations are moving from fulfilling higher needs and going back to the basics.

DOI: 10.4324/9781003018759-8

During the 2020 pandemic the world's population withdrew back to the physiological basics: food, water, safety, and security even to the detriment of our psychological needs to achieve potential. It isn't that we desire to go back to the basic needs, but that's what happens to us when we are met with overwhelming adversity. Whether we experience a global pandemic or a car accident on the way to work, we go back to the basics when we are in a stressful situation. When we are in the middle of a crisis, our bodies simply retreat and shut down all higher order functions. It's difficult to solve genetic problems or negotiate deals when we are skidding toward the edge of a cliff. When we can assure that we are safe, we can begin to rebuild, evolve, and grow from the experience. Stress and worry have a negative impact on mental health and well-being. Individuals, communities, societies, and even governments retreat to physiological needs and shut down higher order psychological needs until health, safety, and security could be restored.

Our workplaces withdraw in the same way as individuals and refocus on the essential (physiological) needs of the organization during an emergency: efficiency and managing cash flow. This keeps the doors open. We go to the survival mode even to the detriment of customer satisfaction and organizational mission.

Humans and organizations are much more alike than we might like to consider. Adversity and self-determined challenges provide us an opportunity to learn, unlearn, evolve, and repeat. Adversity, change, and innovation build our resilience and allow us to learn from the past and to thrive in the future. We learn how to rely on ourselves in our workplace and others to succeed as a team. We learn the relationships that are needed to overcome adversity. Employees are the most essential element of any high-performance organization. The people in our organizations ultimately determine our success or failure.

Our workplaces can be defined in many ways. An image that comes to mind is the organization itself. However, the organization likely includes the monstrosity of all the locations, processes, systems, hierarchy, and people who make up all the international subsidiaries of a global organization. Thinking smaller, you may also imagine a regional office, division, agencies, or your location. It might be smaller still as a single factory, farm, or family store. A workplace is where people perform tasks, projects, and jobs. It may be in a structure, several locations each week, mobile, remotely, or virtual. The workplace provides a space for employees to innovate, create, collaborate, and efficiently deliver their products and services to their customers. Most important is our workplace/organizational community – this is where we have the most impact.

Our Workplace Community

Samuel Jackson states, "To talk in public, to think in solitude, to read and to hear, to inquire and answer inquiries, is the business of a scholar." As a university professor, and scholar, my workplace is where I do work each day. It is where I interact with potential students, my current students, and graduates. It's where I partner with administrators and the staff to recruit, retain, and graduate students. It's where I collaborate with colleagues at universities around the world to prepare students for jobs that are not yet created. It is where I interact throughout the day, week, and year. It's my engaged colleagues that allow me to succeed at my job. At the beginning of my career, my workplace was located brick and mortar, and the students visited during office hours and attended classes, as scheduled, on campus. Today, it's not uncommon to have students, in many different time zones, synchronously or asynchronously attending the same university course. The university has become more virtual over the last 20 years. However, it does very little to change the definition of my workplace. I consider my workplace to be the area that influences my work and that I influence through my work.

In the subject of wisdom, the growth of individuals in the workplace affects the overall health, culture, efficiency, and productivity of the workplace community. As the saying goes, a rising tide lifts all ships. The needs of individual employees and organizations are not dissimilar. Employee health, well-being, and fulfillment affects workplace culture, absenteeism, retention, performance, and everything in between. Ultimately, healthy, fulfilled employees are happier and more productive. The development of ourselves and the development of our workplace communities are parallel in need and, for the most part, they are the same in process. Healthy and fulfilled individuals adapt, grow our resilience, and thrive in adverse and challenging environments. In the same way, healthy, agile organizations readily adapt to chaotic market change.

How do you define your workplace?

People interacting with people influences culture. Organizational culture is impacted at every level and either improved or degraded by our interactions with people. Depending on our position in the organization, influence will vary. The best place to influence the culture of the entire organization is from the top. Most of the organizational culture is nurtured or sickened by division into departments, and the health of the culture in those departments can vary widely. We can affect the culture of our workplace through our interaction with others in the organization and through personal agency. For a moment, imagine your workplace and its culture. Where do you influence? Where do you inspire? Where do you support?

Our workplace community is a group of engaged colleagues who offer mutual support and influence and inspire work within the larger organization. This workplace community can often ignore organizational hierarchy to include the system of diverse individuals that support and grow our personal and professional life.

The following sections describe three major areas where we can focus our efforts at fostering wisdom in our workplaces. There's no need to be a CEO to have impact – we can personally impact our workplaces. We know how to interact with information, we know how to teach and transfer knowledge, but the area of wisdom is left largely untouched by most of social science, education, and HRD. However, it could be argued that we have not yet focused on the subject enough to make an impact. At least we have started.

As a first step, ignore the term "wise" or "wisdom" for a moment and consider the best of your colleagues, leaders, and mentors. What qualities do they individually contribute to the workplace? Consider the collection of your workplace colleagues. What attributes does each person bring to the table? No different from leadership, some people are gifted and can develop higher order characteristics more adeptly than others might.

Where are your mentoring partners? We each have attributes that we contribute to the workforce that fall into the areas of knowledge and experience (implicit and explicit knowledge, perspective, systematic thinking), understanding of self (compassion, drive, belief system), and understanding of others (compassion, inspiration, listener). These are attributes, characteristics, and traits that we can leverage for peer mentoring partnerships. We do not have enough of the wise to mentor us individually, but we do have guideposts to their path. The wise are rare, and the subject of wisdom is not easy. We find wisdom and wise behavior exhibited by our colleagues, leaders, and personal mentors. In our workplace, typically we have individuals that serve in formal leadership roles and those that lead informally that will influence and inspire. We also have our trainers/ teachers, mentors, mentees, mentoring partners, and a vast array of mentoring resources that provide avenues, techniques, and methods to help foster wisdom in the workplace. We need partners in our

Figure 6.1 Three keys: Wisdom constructs.

quest toward wisdom. It's a tough path that few attempt and where fewer find success (Figure 6.1).

Resilience

Born into a clan village in rural South Africa in 1918, Nelson Mandela's South Africa was a hostile and violent environment where a person's skin color impacted every aspect of their life. At age 12 he lost his father and became a ward of the acting King at the Great Palace in Mqhekezweni. He pursued a bachelor's degree but was expelled for joining a student protest. Rather than returning home to enter an arranged marriage, he moved to Johannesburg, the "the city of gold," began his political career and joined the African National Congress (ANC) in 1942 and completed his BA degree in 1943.

In 1948, South African elections changed the landscape with a campaign for racially segregated cities under a policy "apartheid" (apartness). Strict laws were imposed on the black population and Mandela joined the fight against it through the ANC. Blacks and whites were separated, and the black population was treated differently, unfairly, due to the color of their skin. A two-year diploma in law, in addition to his bachelor's degree, provided Mandela an opportunity to practice law in 1952. Black South Africans needed representation due to apartheid laws. In addition, white law firms were too expensive for blacks and often overcharged black clients. Nelson Mandela's fight against apartheid led to bans, arrest, and trials over the next ten years, resulting in his arrest and conviction in 1962. Even as a prisoner, he continued the fight.

In 1963, Mandela and ten others faced the death penalty on charges of sabotage. In his most famous "speech from the dock" in 1964 he declared,

> I have fought against white domination, and I have fought against black domination. I have cherished the ideal of a democratic and free society in which all persons live together in harmony and with equal opportunities. It is an ideal which I hope to live for and to achieve. But if needs be, it is an ideal for which I am prepared to die.

He and seven others were sentenced to life in prison. While in prison, he continued his fight against the brutal minority rule and in 1985 he initiated talks that resulted in a meeting between the minority white apartheid government and the ANC.

Nelson Mandela was released from prison on February 11, 1990 and continued to try to end the minority white rule. Mandela, due his fight against inhuman practices, spent 27 years in prison and changed the history of a country. In 1993, Mandela and then President FW de Klerk were awarded the Nobel Peace Prize. In May 1994, Nelson Mandela became the first democratically elected president of South Africa. Fulfilling his promise, he stepped aside from the presidency after one term. Nelson Mandela is one of the remarkably wise. His story, beyond others, is a story of resilience.

Adversity and challenge have an important role in shaping our belief structure, challenging our multilevel problem-solving skills, strengthening our resolve, building mindfulness, and understanding the role of trust. Adversity comes in many forms from short term and easily overcome to traumatic and life altering.

Resilience is our capacity to adapt and recover from difficult situations, adversity, or challenge. Resilience speaks to our ability to bounce back and grow despite adversity. Resilience is a key component between self-reliance and sound judgment. It provides us the psychological strength and mental reserves to struggle, overcome, recover, learn, evolve, and repeat. Our personal resilience is tested during adverse misfortune such as job loss or change, financial hardship, medical emergencies, divorce, natural disaster, or coping with death. Adversity and self-challenge bring us opportunities to better understand ourselves. Adversity challenges our belief systems, testing our patience and perseverance, and our optimism is stretched to find healthy coping skills that move us from confusion, anger, shame, and grief to charting a course of action toward a positive outcome (Figure 6.2).

Figure 6.2 Resilience key: Wisdom constructs.

Resilience in the face of adversity is a process of adaptation and growth. Adverse circumstances challenge our intellectual ability to overcome. Adversity provides an opportunity for deeper understanding of self. Adversity brings forward the fragility of our existence and allows us to better connect with others encountering adversity in their lives. It often provides humbling experiences allowing us to better understand how to express compassion, empathy, and kindness to others experiencing the same. Overcoming and bouncing back from adverse situations is a key component to fostering wisdom in ourselves and others. We each encounter adversities and adverse fortunes that shape our lives. Adversity, in and of itself, is not a bad thing. Adversity plays an integral role in fostering wisdom, and each of us has at least some experience with adversity.

Resilience is a skill that can be learned, practiced, and improved with time and experience. Our knowledge and experience combined with our self-understanding are foundational to our personal resilience. For the most part, we work on our resilience each day as we move from our comfort zone, past fear, and courageously face a challenge that we must overcome. We each encounter a wide range of stresses as employees and as a workplace. We are accountable for our personal resilience and must practice becoming flexible and resilient.

In general, just like personal wisdom, individual resilience can be cultivated into workplace resilience. Remembering that our workplace simply is a collection of nested individuals working toward shared organization goals; the resilience of the individuals and an optimistic culture provide the foundation of a resilient workforce.

Our relationship with our colleagues is needed to build resilience. Resilience does not mean independence, and it is not the ability to simply ignore adversity, pain, and stress. Resilience is a developmental process of learning to process, recover, and grow in the face of adversity. Our personal community and workplace community both have roles to play in increasing both individual and collective resilience.

Workplace resilience is strengthened through shared values and beliefs systems that can be relied upon and referenced to chart a course of action. These systems provide a steadiness during times of turbulent change. Corporate strategies change and markets are overturned but values and belief systems are designed to remain steady.

A healthy workplace community health provides resilient strength to handle adversity and reduce burnout. Our community buffers the impact of adversity and challenge with optimistic support. When workplace wellness is threatened, it multiplies the negative impact, rather than helping to buffer the impact. Experience and success in adverse situations provide us the opportunity to grow confidence in our ability to overcome future challenges.

Networks support workplace resilience and agility. Individuals and the workplace are better equipped to bounce back from adverse situations when a network of support is in place to support and advise. Our support systems provide an array of opportunities to strengthen our ability to recover from setbacks and challenges.

A well-designed diverse web of colleagues provide mentorship in their areas of expertise and have characteristics that provide flexible support, guidance, and feedback. In addition, these colleagues provide access to new learning opportunities and paths to success.

Shared resilience can improve overall workplace cohesion, empathy, compassion, and performance. A resilient workplace can adapt, recover, and grow in the face of adversity challenges and traumatic change with improved communication to reduce negativity during difficult financial, economic, and dynamic changes. Open communication and shared ideas for recovery and growth can lead to performance innovation and can create a driven and optimistic workforce.

We know that our workplace will have challenges, goals, and pivotal moments. Changing markets and are likely to face catastrophic events that will affect the workplace as a whole and everyone. Our resilience determines our ability to adapt to changes, recover from challenge and adversity, unlearn old models, adapt new models, and grow. Our employees' collective and individual resilience plays a large role in workplace resilience and directly impacts organizational culture.

Adaptability

Rapid change and a global knowledge economy require individuals and organizations to unlearn many old models of work and adapt to new environments and circumstances. Change will happen. With change, we are required to remain agile, adapt, reimagine, revitalize, assess capability and capacity, and strategize an appropriate course of action with shared input.

Adaptability is the ability to agilely adjust to new circumstances. Adaptability is a key to self-reliance and growth. We must be adaptable to survive, and we must be agile to thrive. Adaptability is a key connector between our knowledge and experience and our understanding of others. Adaptability is a skill that can be learned, practiced, and improved with experience. Adaptability improves our flexibility in rapidly adjusting to many new and different situations in life such as change, challenge, environments, cultures, systems, and processes (Figure 6.3).

We each enjoy comfort and sameness. Contentment and comfort lull us into a false sense of security. This contentment in a globally competitive marketplace finds us losing traction to our competitors. Organizations that are weak in innovation, slow to market, struggling in customer support, or producing poor quality products will quickly lose market share. We must be responsive to the pressure of our industries, or we will lose to the innovation of our competitors.

Figure 6.3 Adaptability key: Wisdom constructs.

The Internet has changed everything. Traditional industrial norms simply don't match with a global, hyperinformed, innovative, technological age. Our organization must rapidly adapt to this nonstop change. Information has become accessible and is spreading exponentially. Systems, models, and products are quickly outdated as the market rapidly evolves. The last 30 years have revolutionized how we communicate, share, and interact with each other. Our markets have changed from local to regions to national and international. Our local marketplaces quickly grow to become a globally competitive marketplace, not necessarily by choice, but by customer demand for innovation and accessibility.

In "What Matters Now," Gary Hamel states, "you can't build an adaptable organization without adaptable people--and individuals change only when they have to, or when they want to." The adaptability of our organization depends on the development of an innovative mindset for our workplace communities and individuals. We don't "like" change. Change is an event with a tremendous potential for a negative outcome, and it fills us with a fear of what will come with this change event. Change means moving out of our comfort zone, through fear, to access learning and growth. No matter the possibility of positive learning, growth, and innovation that may be an outcome of this change, we must courageously move through fear to adapt, learn, and unlearn, evolve, and thrive.

Change continues to happen at an ever-increasing pace. In the US, a person will hold an average of 12 jobs between the age of 18 and 50. The World Economic Forum reports that:

> the most in-demand occupations or specialties did not exist 10 or even five years ago, and the pace of change is set to accelerate. By one popular estimate, 65% of children entering primary school today will ultimately end up working in completely new job types that don't yet exist.

The skills and competencies needed for the past 20 years will look distinctly different from the job skills needed during the next 20 years. The need to increase our skill in adaptability to change will increase due to new jobs, new roles, new responsibility, rapid changes in our workplace community, and increasing strategic pivots by organizations to agilely adapt to customer needs. If we are going to change our hiring practices to build a wise workforce, we need to consider several factors to build both capacity and capability. We have to embrace learning, unlearning and an innovation mindset to build our wise workplace communities. We need innovative and resilient individuals that can communicate in a diverse and global community and can agilely adapt to changing circumstances.

As employers, we should seek competent individuals with a generalist attitude and a specialist knowledge. In other words, "the jack-of-all-trades and the master of one." We can predict that our employees will be transient and moving between jobs every 2.5 years. This prescribes that we begin to reexamine the role of the specialist and the role of a generalist. An adaptable employee will have a deep and rich set of primary knowledge and skills within a single job title (master of one) and a generalist (jack-of-all-trades) breadth of secondary knowledge and skills in an occupational category that allows them to nimbly adapt to changing job requirements and global customer demands.

We should seek individuals whose purpose or mission best matches the purpose of the workplace community and organization. When our sense of purpose, belief systems, drive, and compassion are aligned in our personal lives and professional environments, retention rates rise, and personal development and professional development grow together.

We should seek inquisitive learners who have developed their capacity for abstract reasoning, inquisitiveness, self-learning, and unlearning that leads to proactive adaptation in anticipation of changes. These individuals can become our positive disruptors of culture and incubators for innovative ideas and products that anticipate future changes, needs, capabilities, and capacities.

We should seek compassionate and generous individuals with high self-agency that can become an integral part of the workplace culture to help build relationships, reinforcing a mentoring environment for collective growth, overcoming anxiety, stress, and challenges for the purpose of strengthening community resilience. The foundation of the workplace community is growth, shared values, sacrifice, compassion, and empathy.

We should seek kind and ethical leaders that support, influence, and inspire the workplace community. We need formal and informal leaders with the communication skills to listen and ability to foster growth in individuals and the larger community. Our leaders need a strong sense of accountability coupled with knowledge and experience needed to make sound judgments and to chart a strategic and flexible course of action for the community.

The 21st-century employability skills, abilities, and characteristics described above are not a dramatic departure from the employability skills of the last century, and these skills will remain at the core of our lifelong learners. However, technology will further saturate our personal lives and workplaces as access to information and knowledge grows exponentially.

Literacy is a principal skill for agile adaptation and evolution in a global knowledge economy. Literacy has traditionally been considered reading and writing but has been expanded to encompass much more.

Information literacy is our capability and capacity to discover, consume, understand, and utilize information to learn, curate, grow, and communicate (e.g., reading literacy, math literacy, science literacy, media/technology/tool literacy, financial and economic literacy, cultural literacy, and workforce literacy).

Life is a creation, not a discovery. Our knowledge, skills, attitude, drive, persistence, inquisitiveness, creativity, and optimism provide the tools and courage to engage, innovate, and recreate ourselves to thrive in the turbulence of change.

Connection

Connection is a relationship or association between two or more things such as people, groups, community, society, or ideas. Connection is a key to building relationships between ourselves and others. Our social connections contribute a sense of belonging, care, and value by those around us. We can sustain and strengthen ourselves through connection, a basic human need. Our belongingness to a larger community improves motivation, health, and satisfaction and forms the foundation of interpersonal relationships.

As humans, we are uniquely the same, and we are connected. As social primates, we live in complex societies and are gifted with long life and highly developed brains. We rely on cooperation to survive and thrive in the world. Our brains are hardwired to connect with other individuals.

Our personal journey in discovering wisdom is independent of others, but it's not independent of knowing and connecting with others. The view of the wise monk on a mountain is idyllic and provides a wonderful analogy for the wise characteristics such as mindfulness, personal agency, patience, self-growth and self-reliance, and insightfulness. At the same time, understanding of self provides an incomplete picture of wisdom. While the first stage of wisdom may manifest itself as understanding of self, the second stage of wisdom is to understand others (Figure 6.4).

Understanding of others is equally important to the understanding of self. Both are critical for growing in depth and breadth in wisdom. A rich and diverse community of people provides us the opportunity to develop empathy, benevolence, compassion, and generosity for

Figure 6.4 Connection key: Wisdom constructs

individuals, communities, and societies. These characteristics assist us in building connections, developing relationships, and beneficially participating in our community.

Empathy is an ability to understand and identify others' emotions, feelings, and thoughts. While this is not a drive to help, it is a vital first step toward action. This requires an awareness of others and a motivation to understand another's perspective. Empathy allows us to understand how others are feeling so that we can respond appropriately (walk in another person's shoes).

Benevolence is our overall disposition to do good. Benevolence speaks to our inclination to be kind and have a lenient attitude toward others. It is an attitude that guides us to sound judgement and systematic thinking that benefit other people, our community, and greater society.

Compassion is our concern for the suffering of others along with being motivated to help. It allows us to connect and care for each other. Compassion goes beyond having an appreciation of someone's situation to include a move to action with the desire to ease a person's situation. This includes self-compassion. Compassion can increase happiness and optimism and furthers our belief systems.

Generosity is our willingness to freely give our time, presence, and possessions to assist others. Generosity includes overall kindness, selflessness, and giving to others without regret. This selfless attitude of giving has a paradoxical effect of increasing optimism, self-growth, and agency as we connect with others and increase our interaction with our larger community.

These behavioral characteristics provide us with the basic tools to connect with other humans. Our understanding of ourselves and others drive our ability to succeed in a community. When we work and live alone, there is little need to empathize with others or to understand the interconnectedness of a complex social community. All too often, relationship and communication breakdowns can be traced back to compassionate understanding, active listening, and a sympathetic ear. We first need to notice and feel so that we can respond appropriately and begin to develop deeper relationships.

In our workplaces, individuals are often relegated to a singular task or job within the organization with little understanding of how we add to the cohesiveness and performance of the organization. As social primates, we need to have a sense of belonging in our community. Self-directed individuals may understand their purpose, but as a community we must support and assist individuals to find belonging and purpose. This sense of personal belonging and purpose has a positive snowball effect on the health and optimism of our workplace community.

Our workplace communities are living organisms that normally depend on the health of both individual and collective dynamics to function. Our community's health is dependent on our systems of people working together toward a common purpose. The following is an often-told example parable about the power of purpose, but it's rooted in the work of the famous architect Christopher Wren:

> A gentleman strolled down the tree lined street in his small city and rounded the corner to see a brand-new building under construction. In the 1880s, steel had begun to replace wood and stone to erect bridges and buildings and, discovering this new construction site, the man watched three workers in the glow of a setting sun. One was crouched near the bottom of a column, one standing on a scaffold, and one was concentrating and working fast on a stair railing. The curiosity of a new iron building in their city drove the man to ask the questions. He approached the first worker and kindly asked his question, "What are you doing?" The worker looked up at the man and gruffly remarked, "I'm an ironworker. I'm heating the rivets that are to be driven into the holes." Seeing that he was not wanted, he continued to tour and hailed the man standing on the scaffolding, "What are you doing?" The ironworker looked down and responded "I'm a connector. I work with my team to receive the beam and set each in succession." As the ironworker turned to quickly catch and set the next beam and the

gentleman resumed previous meandering. He crossed the building to observe the third working at a furious pace and concentrating on the scrolled railing that led to the side entry of the building. His inquisitiveness moved him to interrupt the ironworker. He asked the same question, "What are you doing?" The ironworker wiped his brow, stood, looked at the sun setting quickly across the building, then inquisitive the gentleman. "I'm a cathedral builder. We're building the cathedral for our families and community."

Each person in our organization and workplace communities inherently assigns a different meaning to their work. A purposeful workplace culture communicates meaning to individuals' roles in their community and creates a complete picture of an individual's role in the vision.

Purpose and connection are powerful and transformative. They can transform a singular purpose of self to a collective purpose.

Communication

Communication is the act of sharing data, information, knowledge, or wisdom from one place, person, or group to another with the purpose of understanding or sharing meaning. Communication allows us to develop shared understanding and meaningful relationships. It allows us to share needs and desires, ask questions, and engage with others. We express our ideas. We have a need to resolve misunderstandings that may cause anger, resentment, or confusion. We assert influence. We inspire others. We use connection to bring people closer to and build community. Finally, we communicate to meet physical and emotional needs of belonging.

At the core of relationships and understanding is communication. At the core of that communication is an interaction between two or more individuals. This interaction has three critical components that work as a system: sending a message, receiving a message and feedback. Our workplace communities are founded on clear communication that focuses on shared purpose, empowerment, support, culture, involvement, trust, connectedness, interaction, identity, and innovation.

Communication happens! Whether positive or negative communication is always happening in complex social communities. As we build connections with individuals and develop relationships, we utilize five types of communication: verbal, nonverbal, visual, written, or listening. Interestingly, listening may be the most important.

If we cannot listen to the person communicating with us, we cannot effectively engage with them. Listening is a surprisingly complicated process involving receiving, understanding, remembering, evaluation, and responding.

In 1987, Futurist Stanley Davis argued the concept of an anytime anyplace economy of the future. In doing so, he accurately predicted an economy created on the foundation of two new modes of communication: any time any place (cell phone, email) communication and mass customized communication (social media) almost two decades later. Cell phones, the internet, and globalization have decreased the time of communication and have created a fantastic array of communication tools moving our global communications away from phone lines and fax machines to an amazing miniature computer that travels with us and allows communication anytime and anyplace on the planes. This singular communication tool created new technological communication barriers to be overcome in a global anytime anyplace workplace community. Today, communication (verbal, nonverbal, visual, written, one-way, and two-way) is limited in some of our common technologies. When we communicate face-to-face, we can utilize verbal, nonverbal, visual, written, one-way, and two-way communication tools that provide a rich conversation for both parties. The World Wide Web, email, and globally connected cellular phones have exponentially increased the speed of communication, introduced new communication platforms, and enabled access to the global population. On the other hand, this speed of communication has multiplied the possibility of miscommunication within our diverse and global workforce.

Organizational communication can be formal, informal, hierarchical, and horizontal with nearly unlimited options and combinations of communication tools. Our technological communication tools allow us to instantaneously communicate with every employee, yet most lack the richness to fully communicate our thoughts and feelings. The danger of our multidimensional communications technology is that we often trade the rich communication dialog and relationship building for the ease and speed of rapid information delivery. Empathy, compassion, and generosity are central to the listening and mentoring processes since they are a direct conduit to our own emotion, thoughts, and feelings that allow us to respond and behave most appropriately to build deeper relationships. We build workplace relationships and culture through our communications. Organizational hierarchies have a history of building silos of communication that move up and down the organizational chain of command rather than across organizational boundaries of departments, roles, job titles, and location.

Belongingness

Belongingness is a human need to give and receive support and provide security as an engaged member of a group. We have an inherent desire to belong to a larger social group. Belonging provides us with an opportunity to be part of something greater than ourselves. A sense of belonging is critical to allow us to engage in with our community and become an integral part of the community's purpose. Inclusion in a community does not denote belonging. Belonging is more powerful and more important than simply being included in the group, community, organization, or society. It implies a greater relationship rather than simple acquaintance, colleague, or familiarity. A sense of belonging and shared purpose has a major impact on performance and retention. When we feel like we don't belong, our performance and personal life suffer.

Individual belonging and engagement as a member of the community will vary based on the individual and organization but belonging and engagement work together. Our level of need for belonging will vary individually, some will be more independent and less engaged. It is the role of the community or communities' formal and informal leader to include the new member and foster belonging to help the person find an engaged role in community purpose. While often this is first based on workplace competencies during the hiring process, this becomes largely a workforce need issue rather than a community need for health and welfare of the culture and health of the community. This secondary role as a member of the community is important for workforce community members finding a sense of belonging rather than simple inclusion due to knowledge or work experience. Belongingness includes engagement in community cohesion in addition to individual and collective community performance goals and outcomes. Belonging does not mean contentment. It means that members are free to speak up, share ideas, act as positive disruptors, participate in mentoring and mentorship, lead, collaborate, and fully contribute to the cohesion, performance, and purpose of the workplace community.

Our workplace communities are where we belong and are engaged. If we are engaged, our role in the community inherently affects the culture, health, and performance of our workplace through support given and received from the community. For a moment, reimagine your workplace and its culture. What is your role in supporting the cohesion of your community? What is your role in supporting the performance of your community? Where do you inspire? Where do you support and need support? If you are an informal or formal leader, do the same for each person in your workplace community.

Start Here

Theodore Roosevelt is famously quoted, though misattributed with "Do what you can, with what you have, where you are." Roosevelt notes that the quote originated from Squire Bill Widener of Widener's Valley, Virginia, in his 1913 autobiography. These wise words have stood the test of time.

Our workplace community is a group of compassionate colleagues who offer mutual support and influence and inspire work within the larger organization. While measures of performance and customer satisfaction are easily quantified, our workplace communities' health and culture are foundational to overall organization success, yet not easily assessed as directly contributing to individual performance outcomes.

Our workplace is where we are. It's where we engage with others and where we belong. Our workplace is a good place to start building individual and collective workplace resilience, adaptability, and connection as keystone factors that connect our three wisdom constructs of "understanding self," "understanding others," and "knowledge and experience." Individual and collective wisdom is both uniquely individual and commonly treasured.

7 Moving to a Wise Workplace

Knowledge is power, while wisdom is freedom.

The world creates approximately three quintillion bytes of data each day, and most of that data have been produced in the last two years. The production of these data may double every two years. Data are everywhere and are the raw material that we use to drive our global knowledge economy. Data are used for information and knowledge.

Data are a collection or set of facts (numbers, work, measurement, observation, or description) that can be quantitative or qualitative in nature. Data, for the most part, are of little help by themselves. We have the task of finding meaning within the data by asking the right questions, collecting data, cleaning the data, analyzing, and interpreting the results.

Information is structured data with attached meaning, connection, and significance. Information forms the basis of our communication. We consume an inordinate amount of information daily in both our personal and professional lives. Information literacy provides the ability to understand and contextualize information to create knowledge. Information literacy is our capability and capacity to discover, consume, understand, and utilize information to learn, curate, grow, and communicate (e.g., reading literacy, math literacy, science literacy, media/technology/tool literacy, financial and economic literacy, cultural literacy, and workforce literacy).

Knowledge is the depth and breadth of information and skills acquired through interaction, participation, and observation integrated with an individual's comprehension of connected experiences. Knowledge can be divided into explicit knowledge (knowledge that others know) and implicit or tacit knowledge (knowledge of things without knowing how you know them). This is often referred to as intuitive knowledge or know-how. This is knowledge that is largely based on

DOI: 10.4324/9781003018759-9

experience, intuition, and insight. Knowledge is a valued commodity that has quickly formed the basis of a globally competitive knowledge economy.

The rapid rise of the global knowledge economy has paralleled the development of the internet. Cellular phone and global workforce connectivity have made information accessible to everyone and communication across the globe a commonplace event. Information is overwhelming and knowledge is common. Competent and experienced employees are not enough. Our best commodity in a competitive knowledge economy is not knowledge, but a wise workforce.

The Role of Wisdom

We cannot expect, and it's likely not possible, that we can teach, train, or even foster everyone in our organization to become wise. To be a wise person is both personal and aspirational. Wisdom is contextual and wise is rare. But understanding and integrating the constructs of wisdom and the characteristics of the wise can leverage human potential or our workplace communities and organizations. These, as explored in Part I, provide guideposts for organizational development and culture.

Wisdom has been approached from many different perspectives and fields. Studying philosophy and the philosopher will provide one view of what wisdom is, while science approaches the subject from very different perspectives. Is one perspective more valid than the other? Absolutely not. Each is a different perspective to view the subject. Wisdom is universally recognized, yet elusive to obtain. Ancient philosophers, such as Aristotle, and modern wisdom scientists struggle to define, understand, or measure wisdom. There is no way to easily understand wisdom without participating in growing your wisdom. Wisdom remains a virtue that can be obtained by anyone.

Wisdom can be defined. We have centuries of definitions and centuries of scholars investigating the subject. Though we may personally struggle to define wisdom, we know it when we see it. Each of us, hopefully, has at least one wise person in our life (personal and professional) to use as a model for how we personally define wisdom. We also have remarkably wise individuals in our communities that can become aspirational models of what wisdom can entail, the wise are the people that we meet every day.

Daryl Davis was born in 1959 in Chicago, USA as the son of a Department of State Foreign Service officer. Due to his father's job, he moved around the world and lived in several different countries. He experienced racism as a 10-year-old when strangers threw glass bottles as he marched in the Cub Scouts parade as the only black child in the den. His parents had explained that these people wanted to hurt him for no other reason than the color of his skin. An avid reader, he learned more about racism in his teens. After graduating Howard University, he became a blues musician playing with Chuck Berry, BB King and others while traveling nationally and internationally. At 25, a chance meeting and a conversation with a KKK member after a gig led to a longer connection and eventually to traveling the country interviewing KKK leaders and members. While writing a book about racism, he interviewed the national Imperial Wizard of the KKK, Roger Kelly. Davis and Kelly developed a friendship that led Roger Kelly to quit the Ku Klux Klan. Upon quitting, he gave Daryl Davis his robe and hood, the robe of the Imperial Wizard. Other previous members have also quit because of Davis's efforts, using his skills of listening, empathy, compassion, sharing, connection, patience, and optimism. His work has led to hundreds leaving their racist organization.

"Wise" is free of discrimination or prejudice. There are no age requirements – wisdom science has provided evidence that there is little correlation between age and wisdom. There is no educational requirement. While some minimal level of knowledge or intelligence is a necessary base to growing wisdom, Intelligent or knowledgeable does not mean wise. There are no race or cultural requirements – we have many references and examples of wisdom (or the wise) across all cultures and throughout time. There is no religious or nonreligious requirement. Religious and nonreligious texts throughout time have studied the topic of wisdom. Wisdom is contextual with a group, community, or society. There is no ownership of the subjects, only lenses that are used to explore and grow in wisdom. There is no nationality requirement for wisdom. Historians of society and linguists can provide evidence of the study and example of wisdom from very simple to very complex societal locations. We find examples of wise people in every culture throughout our human history describing individuals as diverse as our global population. The title of "wise" is not easily earned by individuals. It is bequeathed without regard to age, race, sex, orientation, culture, religious belief, disability, citizenship, political belief, societal condition, or any other classification. It is equally accessible by all.

Wisdom is mutually respected and beneficial to society. The value of wisdom is so overwhelming that individuals ignore and overlook many discriminatory prejudices to seek the wise. In a diverse and globalized world, our understanding and acceptance of others become radically more important. As has been repeated often, we are all uniquely the same.

> *Consider the characteristics of the very best of your PREVIOUS colleagues, employees, or leaders: What do you remember about each of them? Simply consider what made these individuals memorable to you. Create a list of the characteristics that made them special.*
>
> *Consider the characteristics of the very best of your CURRENT leaders, employees, and colleagues: What makes these the best individuals that you work within the organization? In additional Ignore the hierarchical silos of department, division, location, or job title.*
>
> *Create a list of the characteristics and traits that made these people special.*

Your list is likely not exhaustive of knowledge, skills, and competencies of the individuals but describes the person's interaction with their colleagues. Their ability to communicate, interact, support, listen, influence, drive, patience, optimism, compassion, ethics, and responsibility. An individual's competency to perform their job matters; however, it only forms the core of their role in their workplace community. Our interactions with our colleagues, regardless of job title, provide the larger part of our roles as members of our community. Our knowledge and experience span one of three aspects of our workplace role. Imagine a workforce filled with the best of our colleagues.

Every job has requirements (a set of competencies) that must be undertaken to perform efficiently and effectively. We hired people that meet this set of requirements. This set of requirements focuses on what a person can do, rather than how they interact, contribute, and grow. Consider the following job description (modified for anonymity):

Project Manager: This role will use their analytical and organizational skills to support the execution of global projects that improve the clients' capabilities. This role will also utilize their experience to coordinate and/or support cross-functional programs and projects related to manufacturing operations, manufacturing training programs, and manufacturing management.

Role and Responsibilities: Develop insightful recommendations ... Evaluate the impact of proposed changes, with attention to scalability and sustainability ... Create project plans and build consensus ... Coordinate cross-functional projects from outline to implementation ... Support finance coordination ... Keep accurate records and document actions ... Keep ahead of industry's developments and apply best practices ... Adhere to and manage the approved project budget... Design standardized processes and best practices ... Provide key business partners with information and recommendations ... Collaborate with engineering teams as needed ... Develop sustainable best practices ... Take ownership of customers' issues and follow through to resolution.

Experience: A minimum of ten years of experience in project management is required. Proficiency with Microsoft Office suite. Knowledge of process and procedures development. Strong analytical and critical thinking skills. Highly motivated and able to work independently as well as in a team. Strong written and verbal communications skills.

Education: Bachelor's degree in computer science, business administration, project management, or combination of equivalent experience and education required. Master's/Advanced Degree desired.

License or Certification: Desired – Certifications in focused areas such as project management, agile methodologies, or any related industry certifications

Equal Employment Opportunity: We take equal opportunity seriously – by choice.

Though detailed, this hiring description describes only few of the aspects of a person's role in the organization climate, a person's role in personal and professional growth. Personal characteristics and how we are described by our colleagues have much more to do with job satisfaction and job retention than meeting job performance expectations.

Data science, artificial intelligence, and machine learning will have a tremendous impact on how we collect and share knowledge and information and complete performance tasks in organizations. With never-ending data and computing power, we can model and predict future trends with machine learning algorithms that can create models of real life. These models can learn from their own data, learn from mistakes committed, and improve their performance over time, much in the same way humans learn from knowledge and experience. These technologies will have a tremendous impact on the way we do work.

We are paralleling today what we experienced during the industrial revolution with the use of machines to change agrarian society.

In short, we are on the cusp of creating artificial intelligence with deep learning that can mirror cognitive function to create adaptive learning machines capabilities that can self-improve. Natural language processing programs can transcribe to the level of humans and have exceeded humans at chess. Artificial intelligence thrives in a kind learning environment where rules are steady, and feedback is instantaneous and correct. Indeed, computers can become experts. Intelligent automation is just around the corner where knowledge tasks will become more automated, and the human roles may decrease significantly or disappear. The likely shortcoming of computers is lack of virtues that we find in our colleagues: sound and ethical judgment, compassion, engagement, inspiration, courage, respect, sacrifice, creativity, social intelligence, intuition, and empathy.

Our world has significantly changed in the past ten years. Employees struggle to find meaning and purpose in their work. It's no longer enough to just "get a paycheck." As a young and mobile generation, Generation Z is leading efforts to redefine the meaning of work, work location, work culture, work involvement in social change, and what a career means. Generation Z grew up with technology in their hands. The Internet of Things (IoT) has developed during their lifetime. The IoT refers to a network of physical devices that are connected and share data on the internet (e.g., phones, thermostats, wearable devices, RFID tags). This development is enabling them to reshape their work lives.

Finding meaning and purpose in work is important. Finding a shared purpose results in greater retention and employee satisfaction. Organizations, of course, will always target competence when hiring. But we also need to build a workplace that provides connection and purpose, rather than only silos and performance. Culture is founded on the virtues, characteristics, and traits of each person in the workplace community. We need wise individuals that can engage and inspire others in their workplace.

Peter Senge's 1990 book *The Fifth Discipline* popularized the concept of the "learning organization." Senge prescribed that organizations build innovative learning organizations through systems thinking, personal mastery, mental models, building a shared vision, and team learning. Learning organizations are a foundation from which we can build wise organizations. A wise organization is a step forward, as adding "fostering wisdom" is a natural next step in progression of organizational learning and growth.

Collective Wisdom

We can foster wisdom. Windom is obtainable, independently, by every human. As a community of social learners, we can demonstrate, organize, and grow collective wisdom. Our organizations are filled with knowledgeable workers, knowledge management specialists, and human resource development professionals who have long-proven models and methods to transfer information and knowledge. The central idea of building collective wisdom in organizations is to create a better future for their communities.

> *Collective wisdom is a shared understanding of wise behaviors that are collected and curated by an interconnected group to create a beneficial course of action for the group, communities, and society.*

We should seek compassionate and generous individuals with high self-agency who can become an integral part of the workplace culture to help build relationships, reinforcing a mentoring environment for collective growth, and seek to overcome community anxiety, stress, and challenges for the purpose of strengthening community resilience. We must strive for a diverse community that is adaptable and rich in knowledge and collective wisdom. Collective wisdom is not simply shared knowledge and learning, though it's a great start, but building a workforce that learns, adapts, and grows together. Our community should be involved in both individual and collective career development. Our community should be involved in both individual and collective personal development. Our community should create a sense of belonging and shared purpose toward engagement. Finally, our community should develop leaders that inspire and influence toward the community's shared purpose.

The access to information and knowledge is extraordinary. The critical skills needed today are not only job-based technical skills but also career-based soft skills. Well-developed soft skills allow individuals and the larger community to remain flexible and adaptable to changing market conditions. Soft skills and generalist skills will always remain transferable. Training can remedy technical skills and lack of job competencies. However, it's difficult to develop advanced soft skills without an investment in time, energy, mentoring, and education. These skills create our community culture. Workplace community resilience, adaptability, and connection allow our workforce to adapt to changing market conditions and challenges, recover and adapt to adverse conditions, and connect with others who support and advance cohesiveness and performance.

Fostering collective wisdom is an ongoing process. That does not depend on organization profits, market changes, or customer demands. A negative market change is an adversity to overcome. This adversity is an opportunity for growing the collective wisdom of our community for the purpose of strategically planning for the next market loss. We continually grow our capacity and capability by building collective resilience to change. As an organization or community, we build resilience to changes (positive and negative) and learn skills of adaptability to grow and evolve as an organization.

Health and Performance

The analogy to use in imagining the complexity of organizations is the human body. This analogy will only take us so far, but it is especially helpful when we explore wisdom.

Within all our bodies we have five distinct systems: circulatory, nervous, respiratory, digestive, and skeletal. These systems are relatively independent of each other, but they function together for the welfare of the body as a whole. While independent systems in and of themselves, they lack function outside of the organization of the human body. These systems work together to keep our body healthy and functioning so that we can meet our daily activities. For most, this functional body is enough. If we feed and maintain it, it will function.

A traditional hierarchical organization typically has specialized divisions/systems such as marketing, finance, sales, human resources, and operations. These divisions are relatively independent of each other, but they function together for the welfare of the organization. While independent systems in and of themselves, they lack function outside of the business organization. These divisions work together to maintain financial health and satisfy customers. For many organizations, this functional body is enough. If we feed and maintain it, it will function.

Athletes are created from normal people. The functional systems are the same: circulatory, nervous, respiratory, digestive, and skeletal. A normal person becoming an athlete is required to make changes to achieve their goals. Attitude, nutrition, training, investment, and equipment. It's not an easy change, and it doesn't happen overnight. Elite athletes are also created from normal people. Again, the functional systems are the same. The elite athlete also has talents, ability and a skill set that allow them to further excel at even higher goals. This doesn't alleviate the elite athlete from even further optimizing attitudes, nutrition, investment, and systems. Wisdom is not easy, but it's achievable by normal people. Collective wisdom is also achievable by normal organizations. Wise organizations have the same opportunity to achieve a level of performance that is achieved by few, but universally valued.

To be successful in a knowledge economy, we first become a learning organization, then we develop our collective wisdom. When an organization or workplace community is dedicated to a shared purpose, we see a positive effect on individual and collective cohesion and performance.

Culture and Health

Organizational culture defines the shared values, expectations, behaviors, practices, and interactions of an organization. A healthy organizational culture is the key to developing the traits necessary for business success. Healthy culture leads to revenue growth, increases engagement and satisfaction, and reduces turnover. Organizational culture is a dynamic set of patterns, values, behaviors, and perceptions that are learned and shared by a group of people. Leaders, both formal and informal, have a tremendous influence on the culture, organization, systems, and people. Organizational culture is described as a gift when it's positive and a curse when it's negative. Organizational culture is not dichotomous, nor is it an object that we can touch, measure, and manipulate on a day-to-day basis. The following are 12 qualities of culture that optimize our wise organizations:

Ethics are vital to an organization. A trusting culture based on sound ethics is the first step to building shared purpose, engaging employees, and providing a professional climate that invites ideas and connected resilience.

Shared Purpose is a promise/agreement with our collaborative partners. It provides the "why?" of our work. As social creatures it provides us a catalysis for engagement, beyond self, to support and be supported by the community to achieve a common purpose.

Leadership (formal and informal). The best of our leaders influence, inspire, and support their followers. Our leaders are the champions. Leaders are not only a champion of organizational purpose but also equally champions for the ideas and concerns of their followers.

Support is needed for individuals to take risks and provide honest feedback. If trust, ethics, and psychological safety are in question at any level of the organization, individuals cannot feel safe to fully engage and contribute toward a shared purpose. Leadership must take the lead in creating a safe environment where everyone feels comfortable contributing, learning, and developing.

Connection is a key to building relationships between us and others. Individuals must connect both to their colleagues and organizational purpose. We cannot access empathy, compassion, and generosity without a connection to our community and larger organization.

Belongingness is a human need to give and receive support and security as an engaged member of a group. With belonging comes mentoring, development, sacrifice, learning, and growth. I cannot hope to engage individuals that don't feel that they belong – even if they are included.

Positive Disruption is good for the organization. Positive disruptors see opportunities for improvement and move away from groupthink. Collective wisdom is derived from the collective wise behaviors that we have in our organizations. Our positive disruptors look for new ways of doing ordinary things in a more efficient and effective way. We need adaptability, open-mindedness, innovations, and ways to leverage our capabilities and capacities. Wisdom comes from our growth, adaptability, connection, and resilience, not from stagnation and contentment.

Incubator of Innovation is a culture that supports innovative programs at the risk of failure. This innovation can lead to new resources, technologies, markets, and customers. We take risks and get honest feedback from the failures. Innovation at risk to failure can only exist in a safe and engaged culture.

Resilience is our capacity to adapt and recover from difficult situations, adversity, or challenge. If we take risks, we will eventually fail and must learn to bounce back and grow despite adversity. Good judgment comes from overcoming bad experiences and judgments. Resistance to change and failure provide the opportunity for agile change and rapid innovation.

Learning and Unlearning are windows to new knowledge and wisdom. Our models of the world are temporary, and we must become adaptive to change. While we are taught that learning is positive, unlearning is weighing, judging, comparing, discerning, and deciding if a new model or paradigm should replace outdated ones to adapt to new circumstances. As we grow in complex social environments, we learn from rich diverse experiences that challenge our assumptions, and we must be willing to disengage from old models, evolve, and grow.

Systematic thinking allows us to see the processes and diverse communities that span across the hierarchy of the organization to overcome natural barriers to mentorship, learning, efficiency, and effectiveness. It's very easy to see our independent system in the organization and miss how it is interconnected to other systems in the same organization working toward the shared purpose.

Optimism is an attitude that positivity will result from an attitude or an action. Optimism provides more agency because that you are responsible for the positive attitude even in face of challenge and adversity.

People interacting with other people influences culture. Organizational culture is impacted at every level of the organization and either improved or degraded by our interactions with people. Depending on our position in the organization, influence will vary. But every engaged individual has some impact on the organization in a positive or negative direction. The best place to influence the culture of the entire organization is from the top. But most of the organizational culture is nurtured or sickened in the division, departments, system, and communities of the organization with the health of the culture varying widely among areas depending on engagement with the shared purpose. As a wise organization we optimistically and cooperatively learn, adapt, and grow through interaction, participation, and observation with valued members of our social community.

The health of a world-class athlete is primary to their success. Mental and physical strength allow them to push their minds and body to a level beyond their previous standard. The grind of training as working to improve every aspect of their passion can lead to failures, injury, and setback. The reason for injury is not complacency or comfort, but comes from moving beyond their comfort zone to grow. These setbacks test resiliency and require care, recovery, and hard rehab before normal can be achieved again and progress can resume. These athletes strive with an optimistic attitude to reach further, higher, and deeper into their perseverance to achieve a level of performance that they have never seen before. How can you reach for something that you know of without knowing how to achieve it? Certainly, some athletes have talents and abilities that exceed others as do many people in many walks of life. An optimistic attitude, trust, support, innovation, belonging, and engagement move our culture forward to allow the organization to reach, grow, develop, and adapt. We do not know what the future of work will become in the next 5 to 20 years, so we need these characteristics in the community.

Data and information can be harvested for competitive advantage; however, this information and knowledge is of little value if we don't know how to fully use it to strategically move our organization forward. We know that we recruit for knowledge of products, processes, and services. We know through our understanding of learning organizations that we need engaged, innovative, and visionary leaders willing to creatively focus on the surmounting challenges that are currently facing our professions. Organizations that continuously improve, learn, and understand the value of data, information, knowledge, and wisdom can flourish in a chaotic global economy. We do know that wisdom will continue to be a unique human commodity that can become a leverage of innovation in our global knowledge economy.

Final Thoughts

Wisdom is the pinnacle of human cognitive performance.

Thank you for exploring the subject of fostering wisdom.

The remarkably wise leave us in awe of the influential power of the right people, at the right time, demonstrating an overwhelming passion to sacrifice their time and presence in the service of others, even at the risk of their own safety. Anne Frank, Mahatma Gandhi, Martin Luther King, Jr., Nelson Mandela, and Theodore Roosevelt provide us with bright guideposts illuminating the elusive path to wisdom and maybe even enlightenment.

As a professor and scholar of 30 years, my intensive journey to study and better understand wisdom began with a perplexing self-talk. It sounded like this.

> Wisdom is beyond me!?! I've taught teachers how to teach and students how to learn, presented and consulted around the world. I've been a professor and conducted research in career and technical education, training and development, human resource development, workforce development, information science, and knowledge management. Yet, I have no idea how to "teach" someone wisdom.

As a scholar studying human development, career development, learning cognition, and knowledge management, this was a vast black hole of understanding that I had always shied away from for good reason. In all honesty, I'm not sure that I could have explored and understood wisdom 20 years ago. I'm not sure that my depth and breadth of knowledge was rich enough to help myself and others to shine a light into this vast subject.

There are over two millennia of writings about wisdom. Philosophers such as Aristotle, Socrates, and Markus Aurelius have volumes on the subject of wisdom. Yet, in this writing, there is still a lack of agreement on how to teach wisdom. There are a few guiding principles that are evident in as an outcome of this journey:

- Age is not a key. Many people grow old yet are not labeled wise by their peers.
- Intelligence is not a key. There are exponentially more knowledgeable people than wise people.
- Age is not discriminatory. Anyone has the innate ability to achieve wisdom.
- Experience is a key to developing wisdom. But experience needs to be rich, deep, and wide.
- "Wise" is a description that is given by those that they inspire and compassionately support. Wise differs from community to community. A grandmother in Oklahoma, a mentor in London, and a medicine doctor in the Amazon may all be considered equally wise within their circle of influence. Wise is a virtuous title describing the wise people in our life. The definition of wise will equally describe each person.
- Wise is uniquely human. While we can personify the characteristics of the wise to animals, the complexities of wisdom quickly break down and are more akin to intelligence and instinct. Will technology be able to become wisdom? Never.
- The characteristics of the wise vary from person to person and community to community. Yet, a core of characteristics creates a unique composite wisdom for each individual, but never only one characteristic or construct (Knowledge and experience, Understanding of others, Understanding of self).
- Resilience, adaptability, and connection are linking characteristics that tie together the three major constructs and provide insight into how we grow and understand wisdom.
- Challenge and Adversity are critical keys to the development of wisdom. The wise have a resilience to adversity that allows them to grow from the experience and use that experience to their advantage in solving future problems.

- Unwavering optimism is the foundation to growth. A realistic optimism, that despite *difficulty, adverse fortune*, or *challenge*, we can become better through what we know and experience.

I remain convinced that we cannot teach wisdom. Foster or cultivate are much better terms that encompass how we grow wiser. The wise often do not provide "the answer" or solve the problem for you. Rather, they discuss, explore, and provide advice and mentorship on how to solve the problem. Do they teach? Yes, sometimes. Do they coach? Yes, sometimes. Do they advise? Yes, sometimes.

Over and over, there seems to be similar description of the interaction between the wise and those that they foster:

- A compassionate person who gives generously of their time and presence.
- Competence in many areas and a master of one or more.
- An active, inquisitive listener who demonstrates empathy.
- A perceptive and optimistic counselor who can use their personal ethics and belief system to develop trust and find root cause.
- An insightful and intuitive thinker who uses abstract reasoning skills to investigate solutions.
- An objective judge who can see beyond a situation to evaluate the impact of a course of action for the individual and others.

Wisdom has been studied for millennia, and it remains just beyond our collective grasp. I'm privileged to be another on the journey. It's a philosophical question that we cannot quite answer, but it is a path that we can travel as social learners. As we travel our paths, our knowledge and experiences create a picture of understanding. We interact with others, and it inherently changes our perspective, perception, and interpretation of our world. Finally, our quiet introspective reflection cultivates insight and discovery and new growth. Wisdom fosters a better us.

Glossary

Jeff M. Allen https://orcid.org/0000-0003-0551-0539

Adaptability is the ability to agilely adjust to new circumstances. Adaptability is a key to self-reliance and growth.

Agency is your personal level of belief that you are responsible for your own feelings, thoughts, and actions. Rather than other people controlling your feelings, thoughts, and actions.

Belongingness is a human need to give and receive support and security as an engaged member of a group.

Benevolence is our overall disposition to do good. Benevolence speaks to our inclination to be kind and have a lenient attitude toward others.

Collective wisdom is a shared understanding of wise behaviors that are collected and curated by an interconnected group to create a beneficial course of action for the group, communities, and society.

Compassion is our concern for the suffering of others along with being motivated to help.

Connection is a relationship or association between two or more things such as people, groups, or ideas. Connection is a key to building relationships between ourselves and others.

Culture is learned patterns of perception, values, and behaviors, shared by a group of people, that are dynamic and heterogeneous.

Data are a collection or set of facts (numbers, measurements, observations, or descriptions) that can be quantitative or qualitative in nature.

Empathy is an ability to understand and identify others' emotions, feelings, and thoughts.

Explicit knowledge is knowledge that others know. This is often referred to as book knowledge. It is knowledge that can be articulated, documented, and shared efficiently.

Experience   is the practice or the application of knowledge over a period of time.

Generosity   is our willingness to freely give our time, presence, and possession to assist others.

Implicit/Tacit knowledge   is knowledge of things without knowing how you know them. This is often referred to as intuitive knowledge or know-how. This is knowledge that is largely based on experience, intuition, and insight.

Information   is structured data with attached meaning, connection, and significance.

Insight   is sudden understanding of a nonobvious situation or problem by utilizing personal experiences combined with systems understanding, and analysis too.

Intuition   is the ability to make decisions (yes/no) without conscious cognitive reasoning or deliberation.

Knowledge   is the depth and breadth of information and skills acquired through interaction, participation, observation integrated with an individual's comprehension of connected experiences.

Learning   is a natural intellectual process of acquiring and enhancing knowledge, skills, attitudes, and ability through education, observation, self-study, experience, and experimentation.

Literacy   is our capability and capacity to discover, consume, understand, and utilize information to learn, curate, grow, and communicate.

Mentoring   is a guarded two-way relationship, based on mutual trust, between two or more mentoring partners where both members share and nurture growth of knowledge, experiences, and an understanding.

Mentors   are trusted and competent guides that model, listen, foster, influence, and inspire others to achieve a goal or purpose.

Organizational Culture   is a dynamic set of patterns, values, behaviors, and perceptions that are learned and shared by a group of people.

Resilience   is our capacity to adapt and recover from difficult situations, adversity, or challenge. Resilience speaks to our ability to bounce back and grow despite adversity. Resilience is a key between self-reliance and sound judgment.

Sound judgment   is our capability and capacity to objectively draw conclusions based on facts, circumstance, gained knowledge and experience, risk analysis, abstract reasoning, intuition, and systematic thinking.

Tacit/implicit knowledge   *see* implicit knowledge

Unlearning is weighing, judging, comparing, discerning, and deciding if a new model or paradigm should replace outdated ones to adapt to new circumstances.

Wisdom is a uniquely human quality demonstrated through the application of insight, intuition, experience, and sound judgment in conjunction with personal knowledge, skills, attitudes, and abilities to create a beneficial course of action for individuals, communities, and society.

Workplace is where people perform tasks, projects, and jobs.

Workplace community is a group of engaged colleagues that offer mutual support and that influence and inspire work within the larger organization.

Index

Note: *Italic* page numbers refer to figures.

Printed in the United States
by Baker & Taylor Publisher Services